McMAHON!

McMAHON!

JIM McMAHON

with BOB VERDI

Macdonald
Queen Anne Press

A Queen Anne Press BOOK

This edition published by arrangement with
Warner Books Inc., New York.

Published in Great Britain in 1987 by
Queen Anne Press, a division of
Macdonald & Co (Publishers) Ltd
3rd Floor
Greater London House
Hampstead Road
London NW1 7QX

A BPCC plc Company

British Library Cataloguing in Publication Data

McMahon, Jim
McMahon!
1. McMahon, Jim 2. Football players—
United States—Biography
I. Title II. Verdi, Bob
796.332'092'4 GV939.M36

ISBN 0-356-14215-9

Reproduced, printed and bound in Great Britain by
Hazell Watson & Viney Limited,
Member of the BPCC Group,
Aylesbury, Bucks

To my family, for putting up with me.

J.M.

I would like to acknowledge the help of Bob Verdi, who found the right words, Steve Zucker, for his guidance and friendship, and my teammates and coaches. You guys made it all possible.

J.M.

CONTENTS

FOREWORD

When I first encountered Jim McMahon, I didn't especially like him. I definitely felt the same way the second time, and probably the third, too. I was, and still am, a sports columnist for the *Chicago Tribune*. He was—and of course, is still very much so—quarterback for the Chicago Bears.

The prospect of us collaborating on one interview—let alone several interviews—for the purposes of producing the book you now hold in your hands seemed remote. I am a member of the media, and proud of it. McMahon is a member of the sweat set, and proud of it. In case you haven't noticed, our two professions have developed what politely might be described as a growing adversarial relationship in recent years.

McMahon, not unlike many athletes, regards journalists —print and electronic—with a certain degree of dismay, or at least, distrust. What separates McMahon from many of his contemporaries is that he is utterly unafraid of conveying his feelings toward us. When he doesn't care to be on stage, you might as well turn out the lights.

"You're doing a book with him? Why, he's the biggest jerk I've met in sports in the last twenty years."

A veteran columnist I know well and respect immensely whispered that in my ear during Super Bowl XX week in New Orleans last January. My friend had witnessed several days of Jim McMahon, on stage, when Jim McMahon didn't want to be there. It wasn't always a convivial experience, but it was absolutely, positively Jim McMahon.

However, I wouldn't be at all surprised if, in time, McMahon wears a lot better with my fellow newspaperman, just as McMahon has come to wear with me. I can't trace our coexistence exactly, other than to recall vaguely that one of the initial occasions involving any prolonged contact was during a golf tournament, in the same foursome. That provided some sort of common bond, and when we both chose to wash away bad scores with a beer or three, I suppose each of us realized the other had at least a couple redeeming qualities. If, indeed, flogging a golf ball in the name of relaxation can be construed as worthwhile. More important, though, I figured that any doubts about McMahon as a person—not a football player—might best be resolved by observing those who saw him a lot more often, and knew him a lot better. What I discovered was that his teammates and friends, many of whom were both, would kill for him. This kind of ringing endorsement is not to be taken blithely, especially considering that sports teams contain as many jealousies, petty disagreements, and cases of outright dislike as exist in any office of any company.

"I would jump in front of a runaway bus for that guy," says Jay Hilgenberg, an All-Pro center for the Bears. Strange, it is, that so many people feel that way about McMahon. Stranger yet, I think, that so many people wish McMahon would jump in front of a runaway bus. He tends to inspire—maybe even encourage—that dichotomy of emotions, and I don't know of any better way to explain why than to borrow from the man himself. Simply put, McMahon can't do too much for the people he enjoys and can't do too little for the people he doesn't know—or, more significantly, the people he knows he doesn't want to know.

Someone evoking so many different opinions is destined to be perceived as mysterious or enigmatic, and I don't for a minute think McMahon minds being that. But we should not confuse that persona with being two-faced, or political in nature, or devious. On the contrary, McMahon is right there for the taking. With him, you know exactly where you stand, or fall. He is on Monday what he will be on Tuesday and on Wednesday, too. You can depend on that, like it or not.

Of course, McMahon is particularly reliable as a quarterback. At Brigham Young University, he merely became the most prolific passer in college football history. Once upon a time, Tony Dorsett and Ed Marinaro shared the mark for most individual records in National Collegiate Athletic Association annals, 18. When McMahon departed BYU, he had 55.

"Someday," said Brigham Young coach LaVell Edwards, "he will win a Super Bowl for somebody."

The Bears, who had been having problems with the quarterback position almost since the advent of color television, selected him, despite suggestions that he was too small, too fragile, too iconoclastic, what have you. Within four years, indeed, the Bears won a Super Bowl and I'm not revealing any secrets when I say that his teammates credit McMahon with the necessary leadership. He is unconventional, true, on and off the field, but as Mike Ditka—the very head coach McMahon often baffles—says, "Jim's a winner."

McMahon's first reaction to a book proposal was interesting. "Isn't it a little early for that?" he said. Though some detractors would criticize McMahon for being cocky to a fault and self-impressed to the limit, I think he was telling us that, at twenty-six, he had not nearly fulfilled his goals. He really did not think he was the greatest thing since sliced bread.

However, McMahon does believe that he has been grossly misunderstood and misrepresented. After so many skewed pictures of him had been tendered, perhaps he decided it was time to say his piece, in his words, in his book. For all his apparent brashness, McMahon had to be convinced into thinking he was important enough to utter sixty thousand or so words and have them bound.

Given his fame, the demands on his time, and the plethora of companies begging to pay him huge sums to endorse this or that, I would say that this book was among the least profitable of the many proposals before him. And probably the least appealing, because Jim McMahon's favorite subject is not necessarily Jim McMahon.

But, the man who can't sit still sat still for hours upon hours of taping. When there was still snow outside his suburban Chicago home, he cancelled a week's all-expense-paid trip to Hawaii for the family so he could bare his soul. There were mornings when I feared to show up and find a note on his door: "Book Postponed, Gone to Maui for Golf. Couldn't Stand This Weather Anymore. Hope You Understand. Will Have a Cocktail for You. Cheers, Jim."

But he was there, every day, all day, if needed. I'll leave it to the reader to judge content and style, but I think you might be surprised to learn that the "punk rocker" with the shades and the sly smile is really a quite sincere person, gifted with more than a strong right arm. If quick wit is a sign of intelligence, as I believe it is, then McMahon is as bright as he is controversial. He might make some people angry, but I think he makes even more people laugh. Often, the target of his one-liner is himself. In the end, perhaps, the only thing McMahon takes seriously is enjoying life—not a bad game plan, at that.

Selfishly, I wish that McMahon would be more tolerant

with those of us who don't ask to befriend him, only interview him, as part of the job. I think it's part of his job, and we'll argue about that ad infinitum. I don't expect to win, especially because, every so often, he'll be in the mood to let it all hang out.

"Aren't I good copy?" he'll say.

But, of course, he is. Better yet, from the outside looking in, I'm inclined to agree with his friends, that Jim McMahon is an eminently decent person. I can't ever remember seeing him reject an autograph request from a youngster, nor can I ever remember him not melting when either of his children, Ashley or Sean, walked into the room. McMahon's soft spot is there; it's just that he'll decide whether you're allowed to find it. Become one of the chosen few, and what's his is yours.

McMahon's "bad boy" image is largely a result of desire to do it his way. But—and he discusses the subject in upcoming pages—if what he does doesn't hurt anybody, what, then, makes it all that bad? Being a little outrageous is diametrically opposed to being a lot malicious, and McMahon has given too much of himself to others to qualify as anything less than loyal, if not popular. "I don't want to be thought of as a nice guy," he says. "I want to be thought of as a good guy."

My hunch is that you, too, will come to regard him as such. All you have to realize is that the man is himself, and that he's not about to apologize for it. But, it might take a little time. I speak from experience.

—Bob Verdi
June 1986

ONE

Is It Blue?

I'm not much of a detail guy, so I'm sure it didn't surprise my wife, Nancy. She thinks I'm losing a few of my marbles, so she couldn't have been shocked when I telephoned to tell her I'd lost something else, too.

"Nance," I said. "Is there anything lying around the house that looks like a playbook?"

Pause.

"Is it blue?" she answered.

"It's blue," I said. "Where did I leave it?"

"It's sitting here on the kitchen counter . . . right by the stove," she said.

"Oh," I said. "Well, whatever you do, don't barbecue it. See you when you get down here. Bye."

A fine start to the week. There I was in New Orleans, just after arriving on a Monday night, and I'd left my game plan, my visual aids, the whole thing, back home in Chicago. Not unusual for me, but still not a good idea with Super Bowl XX only six days away. Go Bears.

To top it off, or to bottom it off, I had a sore ass. I could hardly walk, let alone do the "Super Bowl Shuffle." I'd been speared in the left cheek during our victory over the Los Angeles Rams for the National Football Conference Championship. I thought it would be better after a week's rest. It wasn't. I couldn't tell what it looked like because, like George Brett said when he had hemorrhoids during the World Series, all my problems were behind me. My roommate, Kurt Becker, who probably sees more of me than he cares to, said it looked like somebody used my butt to finger-paint on. One of the reporters said that all the bruises and welts made it look like a "mosaic," which sounded a lot better than it felt.

"It'll go perfect with your purple bikini underwear," said Becker, an upbeat sort of guy.

"At least I didn't forget *those*," I said.

Actually, I wasn't all that worried about not having my playbook. We'd been practicing since July, and here it was late January. If I didn't have an idea of what the Bears wanted to do to beat the New England Patriots, I'd have to have been even crazier than most people think I am. Besides, at this point, after eighteen games, leading up to the big one, I knew it would be more a game of emotion than strategy.

I had no doubts in my mind that we would win. A few bad dreams, maybe, about playing a bad game at quarterback and losing in a big upset and being blamed for it by all my friends in the press. But, that was about all.

Like most of the Bears, I was hoping we'd play Miami in the Super Bowl. The Dolphins beat us during the regular season, spoiling our chances of having an unbeaten record. We'd have really liked another shot at them. But New England beat Miami in the playoffs. The Los Angeles Raiders would have been nice, too. They were a lot like us: rough; physical; nuts. That would have been a real slugfest. But New England beat them in the playoffs, too.

We really didn't have a case of the "hates" for the Patriots like we did for Miami or the Raiders or Dallas, but we had to respect them. We were 11-point favorites to beat the Patriots, which is a lot. If I had been a betting man, I might have taken those odds, too, the way New England was playing. Three straight wins on the road to get to New Orleans. They had to be good. We played the Patriots in the second game of the regular season, and by no means dominated them.

But, we were better and we knew it. And I knew, if I was healthy enough to play, basically what I would have to do. The rest, I could wing. Becker, a big offensive lineman who wasn't on our active list for the Super Bowl, brought his playbook, but I never bothered studying it. Throw and throw deep. I knew we'd have to make big plays because, of course, this was a big game. The biggest of them all, my media pals called it.

And to hear some of the sportscasters from Chicago talk, you would have thought we were going to take the biggest fall of them all. They kept bringing up the 1963 Bears, and how great they were when they won the NFL title. And we kept hearing about the 1969 Cubs and the 1984 Cubs, who were supposed to win and didn't. And DePaul and the White Sox and the Black Hawks. All Chicago teams that had gotten everybody excited at one time or another, then failed.

The negative thinkers forgot one thing. We were the 1985 Chicago Bears. We weren't anybody else. We were the best team in football all year, and we weren't going to choke like the media thought we would. We didn't want to just beat the Patriots, we wanted to blow them out, humiliate them, embarrass them. And we did, as promised. It's one thing to say you're going to do something. It's another thing to say it, then do it, right?

Game day. Sore butt or not, I slept until about eleven-thirty in the morning, still a long ways before game time. I went downstairs to our team meal at the New Orleans Hilton, and saw the usual eggs and potatoes and lasagna. I'd been getting the idea all week that the Super Bowl wasn't all it was cracked up to be, and this was another indication. Here we were, supposedly the biggest day of our lives, supposedly the biggest meal of our lives, and they're feeding us scrambled eggs and lasagna. Gourmet dining. Management must have gotten a deal on the food.

I took a pass, caught a cab, and got to the Louisiana Superdome, a couple miles away, about twelve-thirty. Matt Ditka, the son of our head coach, Mike, was there, and I sent him out to get a Wendy's burger—no fries; too much cholesterol. I didn't even finish it. That was my pre-Super super meal. Half a Wendy's burger. I never eat much before a game anyway, and not because I'm nervous. And, obviously, not because I'm busy studying the plays, either.

Pretty soon, some of the guys started trickling in. Walter Payton, the legend of a running back, listened to music by his locker. Steve McMichael, alias "Mongo" or "Ming the Merciless," was running around yelling, "Kill the ———!" I could tell then we were pretty loose, just like we were all season. This was no big deal, no reason to change our demented attitudes. We had better talent, better people, *sicker* people than New England.

Mike Ditka then came in and went around the room, talking it up. I don't usually listen to all of what he says. In one ear and out the other. We call him "Sybil," after the girl in that movie. You know, the one who had all those different personalities? Mike will be calm one minute, then throw a clipboard the next. People don't understand that, but we do. The players figure he's just going from one stage to another. He's merely "Sybilizing."

Anyway, Mike came in and lectured us on how we'd been talking all year and talking all week about how good we were. Now was the time to prove we weren't just prima donnas and all that stuff. Otis Wilson, our Pro Bowl linebacker, looked up and told Ditka to relax. It's in the bag, Otis said. We're going to murder these guys. That's how uptight we were. Like Payton says, if they ever want to cast another version of *One Flew Over the Cuckoo's Nest*, they don't have to consult Hollywood. All they have to do is go to the Bears' locker room.

I didn't do much hollering before the game. I never do. I took a shot to kill the pain in my butt, which was only fitting, because I'd been taking needles from the media all week. I sorted out the headbands I was going to wear during the game. I also noticed an article someone had taped to my locker. "McMahon Crybaby!" It was by Dick Young of the *New York Post*. I'd met him before and thought he was a pretty reasonable guy, but now he was ripping me for complaining about the hit I took against the Rams that gave me my sore buns. Young was saying that I couldn't take pain. What game had he been watching? That's all I do is take pain! I love pain! Maybe I should have asked him up to my room one night and showed him my "mosaic." Did he think I needed an injection to cure the common cold?

Finally, it was game time. No more waiting around. We won the coin toss and elected to receive. Everything was going perfectly . . . until the second play. I called the wrong formation, Payton got blasted, he fumbled, and the Patriots recovered the ball at our 19-yard line. I wondered how my playbook felt, lying there on the kitchen counter back home. It was my fault, what happened. New England couldn't move the ball, but they kicked a field goal and it was 3–0 Patriots after two minutes. Those sportscasters from Chicago must have been getting the shovels out. They carry their shovels with them, you know.

Were we worried? The Bears, worried? Are you kidding? We took the ball on the next drive and went right down the field to tie it on Kevin Butler's field goal. I threw one long pass in that first series, hitting Willie Gault for 43 yards. It was a play-action pass, and we were taking advantage of their defensive backs, who were what we call "peekers." When we lined up, they watched our backfield, and wide receivers, to try to get an idea what we might be doing on the next play. It's a good idea, if you can keep all that in your field of vision before you commit, but you can peek too long with a guy of Willie's speed. You can get burned, badly.

I knew then we were going to be able to move on them whenever we wanted. The Patriots were conservative; they didn't blitz much. That's the way they'd played it all year, and they weren't going to change now. Also, they were keying on Payton. That was obvious. But, they spent so much time thinking about him, it was like they forgot the rest of us. Perfect. Perfect for the Bears, anyway. We weren't concerned about their down linemen because we felt we had the people up front who could handle them. And Andre Tippett, their big rush guy on defense, I could see him all afternoon out of the corner of my eye. He didn't do much, or wasn't able to, because we were just too strong, and wanted it too badly. He'd had a bunch of sacks during the season, but he wasn't a factor in the Super Bowl.

None of them were. I respected the Patriots a lot more before the game than after, and not because we destroyed them. There was one play on that first drive by us, leading up to the field goal. I ran with the ball for a short gain and really got crushed by Ronnie Lippett, their cornerback. It was wild. I got flipped up in the air and over. I didn't know where I was for a while, and when I landed, I thought two things. First, I was glad I hadn't let go of the ball. Second, if I hadn't taken acupuncture treatments all week, my behind would have been so sore again, I might not have continued playing. Or, if I had continued, I wouldn't have been worth much. I would have limped through the rest of the game, at best.

As it was, we had the ball at their 10. It was a good, clean hit by Lippett, which was fine. But then he started jumping around all excited, and yapping. They were a little lippy right after they recovered that fumble by Payton, in fact, but now they were really getting out of hand, pointing fingers and swearing and telling us they were going to hurt us.

Not a good idea by them. The Bears don't get intimidated, verbally or physically. We like to play good, hard football and we're not much for debates—unless provoked. Well, that might have provoked us, all the Patriots running around acting like schoolkids. They weren't going to beat us that day even if they minded their manners and said their prayers and brushed their teeth after every play. But when they began mouthing off in the first few minutes . . . well, hell, who do these guys think they are? They might have been aggressive, but they didn't belong on the same field with us.

As the first quarter went on, we got the idea that we could do whatever we wanted. The defense began coming in on their quarterback, Tony Eason, in waves. McMichael and Richard Dent sandwiched him deep in their territory, and Dan Hampton fell on the ball for us. Butler kicked another field goal and it was 6–3.

On the first play after the kickoff, Dent surrounded Craig James, and he fumbled. That was at their 13. Matt Suhey scored for us and we were up 13–3 after the first quarter. I really thought the game was pretty much over then, because I knew our defense had their number. We were like sharks all season. When we smelled blood, we got really excited. We smelled blood early in Super Bowl XX, and the Patriots knew it.

We went 59 yards for a touchdown early in the second quarter, and were driving again just before the half ended. We had run out of time-outs when I scrambled to their 3. There was another shoving match between Keith Van Horne and Fred Marion of the Patriots, but with the clock ticking, I wanted to stop it. We snapped the ball, and I threw it into the ground in the right flat. We got an illegal procedure penalty, but we still had three seconds left. Butler was good again. Now we were up 23–3. Later, the league ruled that

Red Cashion, the referee, had made a mistake. We forced the action to stop the clock by putting the ball in play with less than ten seconds left. The field goal was illegal. Hell, we forced the action all year. *We* should have been declared illegal, we were so good. "Only thirty more minutes till we get our rings!"

That's all I could think about going to the locker room. I might even have yelled that. That's what you play for most, besides the idea of being champions. The Super Bowl rings, not the money. Our only doubts then were about the rings themselves. Management can cut corners if it wants, and knowing the people who run our team don't exactly spend wildly, we figured our rings would be something like those toys you find in the bottom of Cracker Jack boxes.

The second half was more of the same. I passed 60 yards to Gault from deep in our territory the first time we had the ball, and then I scored a couple minutes later from the 1 to make it 30–3. If the Patriots hadn't gotten the message by then, they weren't awake. What did they have, −19 yards at halftime? Eason looked confused and frustrated. He wondered who was going to hit him next and how hard. I know. I've been there. It's not so much that you're afraid to get hit; it's that you know you're going to get killed, no matter what you do. It's not going to work.

Steve Grogan replaced him in the third quarter. I don't think Eason asked to come out. You'd have to be a wimp to want that, and Eason's not a wimp. He probably just wanted to get out of there alive and go home in one piece. They couldn't do anything. It turned out to be the most lopsided Super Bowl ever, 46–10. And to show you how ornery our guys on defense are, they were mad that New England got 10. If the Patriots hadn't have scored that early 3, they'd have probably wound up with 0 because when they got their consolation touchdown, early in the fourth quarter, most of our reserves were in.

I was out of there by then, too. Steve Fuller came in for me at quarterback, and eventually our third stringer, too, Mike Tomczak. It was getting like an exhibition game. I would have liked to keep playing, but when Fuller came in, I went over to Ditka at the sidelines, stuck out my hand, and just said, "Congratulations." His mind had to be going a mile a minute. Then I went over and just stood around, laughing with most of the other guys, waiting for the thing to get over with. A long game, a long season, about to end.

"I'm getting thirsty," said Van Horne, one of my night-crawling pals.

"I'm always thirsty," I said.

If there was one thing I felt bad about at the Super Bowl, it was that Payton didn't score a touchdown. Wally had been playing for eleven years, with some rotten Bear teams, living for this moment, and he didn't get to score. He was one guy who wasn't laughing afterward, and some people assumed he was pouting. I didn't think that. Wally had been the focal point of the Bears for so long. Maybe that's what bothered him. Here was the Super Bowl and we won by 46–10 and he wasn't at center stage. He finished with only 61 yards in 22 carries.

If he'd have had a great day rushing, like 150 yards, it might not have hurt him so badly, not scoring. I don't know. I do know it proved what we'd shown as a team all season long, that we weren't just Walter Payton anymore. That old theory about how if you stop Wally, you stop the Bears was gone. Which is one reason why we became champions.

I also know that anybody who said Wally had nothing to do with the outcome doesn't know football. His mere presence helped the offense. The Patriots were so geared to shutting him down that they let the rest of us go bananas. Havoc! That's how great an effect a Payton can have on a game, even a game where he doesn't come up with the big statistics.

Still, he didn't score, and he felt bad about it. I don't blame him. We could have done something for him, and I'm partly at fault there. I went for one touchdown from the 2 midway in the second quarter. It was an option play; either Wally would get it or me. He came around for the pitchout, but they smelled it coming, so I found the lane and felt I did what I was supposed to do.

In the third quarter, when I scored my second touchdown, the Patriots were waiting for William "Refrigerator" Perry to get the ball. Yeah, he was in our offense by then, too. But their linebackers were sitting over our backs, and nobody was over me. With the linemen down that low, it was the safe call, the easy call, for the quarterback to take it in.

Where I screwed up was when we gave the ball to "The Fridge" about four minutes later. He scored from the 1 to make it 44–3. Ditka got caught up a little too much in his innovations here. He'd made a star out of this big rookie defensive tackle; made him into a touchdown hero. Now, Ditka wanted him to become president of the United States, too. So, Ditka called for Perry to get the ball, and that's where I should have just given it to Wally and the hell with what Ditka wanted.

Thing was, at halftime, Ditka was screaming about how if we could get 60 points, go get them. The way things were going, I thought there'd be plenty more chances for Wally to score. I thought for sure he'd get a shot. I thought I could give him a shot. But, then I got taken out, and we started doing some stupid things. Like throwing the ball. Like running Wally on a 4th-and-goal draw play from their 11. It wasn't Fuller's fault, though, that Wally didn't score. It was my fault. But I still think Wally will get a chance to score in a Super Bowl. He'll get his opportunity.

"So, this is what we worked our asses off for?" I said to Wally along our bench in the closing minutes.

"Yeah, this is it," he said.

We were all kind of quiet after it was over. It was sort of a letdown, kind of anticlimactic. Maybe we'd have been more charged up if we'd won 14–13, but I'm not complaining. I'm just saying it was all a bore. I never thought I'd say that, but it was. I'm no authority on Super Bowls, of course, because this one was my first. But, it seems to me that these games are more for the fans and media: all the hoopla and parties, everybody with a place to hang out—Bourbon Street. I just wanted to play the thing, get it over with, and bolt town.

Late in the game, it was announced that Dent had been voted Super Bowl Most Valuable Player. He had a sensational game: one and a half sacks and two forced fumbles that turned into scores for us. He had nine sacks in three post-season games! He was great. He was great all year. It was mentioned to me that I could have had MVP, with twelve completions in twenty attempts for 256 yards. We'd scored 46 points, I'd scored twice; I felt I'd played well. I also could have thrown a couple interceptions, but got lucky. I knew, though, that the press was voting on the award, and I'd have had to play the greatest game in the history of football to get their votes. Maybe 600 yards in the air? As it was, I was told I got three votes, probably none from the Chicago writers. But it didn't matter. Dent deserved it. Besides, let the clock run out! This game was lasting four hours!

After it ended, I ducked into the trainers' quarters, then took a shower and came back into the locker room, which was pretty reserved. Michael McCaskey, the Bears' president, was skipping around with the Lombardi Trophy in his hands—that's the award you get for winning the Super Bowl. I doubt that he's let go of that thing to this day. He probably sleeps with it.

I grabbed a beer and went through one more of those mass interview sessions. I tried to find Nancy anywhere in the area, but she'd gone back to the hotel. So, I made my way through the mobs and jumped on the team bus. I looked at the Superdome and realized I'd probably never be surrounded by those same three thousand reporters ever again in my life, but, who said life was fair? You have to take the good with the bad, right?

When I got back to my room, Becker and his fiancée were there. Then Nancy, then more and more players arrived. We sat around having a few beers, and then we went from room to room, talking about what a bore the game was, but how glad we were we won this time because of the situation on our team. A lot of guys were unhappy with the front office, so, we figured, it was a good thing we won now, because this thing could explode in another year.

I never even went out of the hotel that night. Most of us just hung around our rooms. We ordered some more beer and pizza. I was tired, drained, but I don't remember getting any sleep. Course, there are a lot of things I don't remember, like my playbook.

But, at least it was over. The next morning, most of my teammates headed back to Chicago for a parade. I wanted to be part of it, because I've never been in one of those ticker-tape jobs. You see them on TV; you wonder what it would be like to be in one. But, it turned out bad. The weather was freezing in Chicago, there were too many people, and the thing wasn't very organized. I guess you can understand why. The Bears didn't have much experience at running parades.

I felt brutal the morning after, but at least I got on a plane for Honolulu and the Pro Bowl game. I didn't feel all that much like a Super Bowl quarterback; I wasn't even going to start in the Pro Bowl. Phil Simms of the Giants did. No problem. I was headed away from all the commotion and toward the warm weather. I had been wanting to play my favorite sport, golf, for the longest while, and now it was time.

I might forget my playbook, but I never forget my clubs. Aloha.

T W O

My Behind, and My Buddy

We were like caged animals leading up to the Super Bowl. Come to think of it, we were like caged animals all season, but especially heading into New Orleans. We played well in the playoffs, beating the Giants 21–0, then the Rams 24–0. We could have played New England the next day after we played Los Angeles. Instead, we had to wait two weeks. League rules.

I'd be in favor of waiting just one, but I guess the league needs the time to organize all those parties for the press. Besides, in my case, the rest did me good. Remember, I had my very own mosaic to worry about.

A few days after we beat the Rams, we went down to Champaign, Illinois, to work out. That's the home of the University of Illinois. They have a nice indoor facility covered by a "bubble," which you need at that time of winter. The University of Illinois football team can afford to have one, but the Bears can't. They only make $17 million from the TV networks every season. You figure it out. So there we were in Champaign, which was really exciting. I expect I'll go back there on vacation sometime.

I certainly didn't go there to practice for the Super Bowl. I was really having trouble moving around with the injury. I hardly did anything all week. Pretty soon, we were back in Chicago getting ready to fly to New Orleans, and it was still a big deal for me to get out of bed. My butt kept hurting, no matter how much time I spent getting treatments or in the whirlpool.

That's where Hiroshi Shiriashi came into my life. Willie Gault mentioned that he was having him fly into Chicago from Tokyo to give him acupuncture. Willie had been fighting aches and pains, and I had no hang-ups about acupuncture. I'd used it often when I was playing college football at my beloved alma mater, Brigham Young University. Why not now, with the Super Bowl right around the corner?

On Monday morning of Super Bowl week, I was still in so much pain that Nancy had to help me put on my socks. I couldn't bend over. Going to the bathroom was an adventure I'd rather not discuss. So, I went up to our training camp in Lake Forest—Halas Hall, named after the late George S. Halas, founder of the Bears, founder of the N.F.L. Papa Bear.

Hiroshi had arrived. I went right into our training room, stripped down, and let him have me. I have no idea why sticking a bunch of little needles in somebody's affected area relieves pain and pressure. I'm not a doctor. I'm not even Japanese. All I know is that it works, and I was glad to hear Willie say that Hiroshi would be coming down to New Orleans with us.

Mike Ditka was all for it. So was Jerry Vainisi, the Bears' general manager. Only one holdup. When Michael McCaskey heard about it, he hit the ceiling of his ivory tower. I had nothing to do with the conversation, but I understand McCaskey got into a pretty nice argument with Willie about club policy.

"Let's get one thing straight," McCaskey said, according

to Willie. "This isn't Jerry Vainisi's team. This isn't Mike Ditka's team. I'm running the Chicago Bears."

In other words, McCaskey didn't want any part of Hiroshi. We found that out for sure when we gathered at O'Hare Airport Monday afternoon for our charter flight to New Orleans. Hiroshi showed up with his grab bag of needles or whatever, and McCaskey said he couldn't come with us. Typical. Was I ever hot!

On the ride down, Willie and I decided that Hiroshi was going to come to New Orleans, even if we had to pay for his ticket and his room. It didn't matter how many yen it would cost us. We wanted Dr. No there.

When we landed, I was still angry, and—wouldn't you know it?—one of the first items on my agenda was to appear at a press conference, one of several such gang bangs on the week's schedule. They brought a bunch of us players into this ballroom at the Hilton, put us each at a seat on a platform, and let the press fire away. Far be it from me to hold anything in. I told the whole story. How I had taken one acupuncture treatment already, earlier that day. How Ditka and Vainisi had approved it because they were for whatever was good for the team. And how McCaskey had scotched the whole thing, because *he* and only *he* ran the Chicago Bears. As I related my tale, the crowd of reporters around me swelled. You've seen that movie *The Blob*? Where this thing just multiplies before your eyes? That was my acupuncture audience.

Well, it became instant news. I had no idea it would become such a big item. All of a sudden, my rear end was the hottest topic of conversation on Bourbon Street. Naturally, my degenerate teammates got into the act.

"You've got the most talked-about ass since Bo Derek," suggested Kevin Butler.

"Are you going to take all this abuse sitting down?" asked Keith Van Horne. "After seeing you in the shower, I guess you can't."

The guys were loving it, but they were also mad. Mad at

McCaskey, which was pretty much how we went through the whole season. I was madder than all of them, of course, because Dr. No was back there in Chicago. For all I knew, he was probably still standing around O'Hare, wondering when the plane was supposed to leave for New Orleans.

I ran into McCaskey at practice Tuesday, and he asked me how things were going, how I felt. That was all I needed.

"I feel brutal," I said, "and if you want me to play Sunday, you better let that guy come in here and work on me."

Of course, it was out of McCaskey's hands now, and he knew it. The Illinois Acupuncture Association had read about the fuss back in Chicago, and they announced plans to foot the bill for Hiroshi to fly to New Orleans. It was the greatest thing to happen to acupuncture since the invention of pain. Hiroshi was on his way, one way or another.

McCaskey finally realized this, and all of a sudden, he changed his tune. Now, he was all for it. He said he was never actually opposed to it; he would be glad to have Hiroshi help out. It's just that McCaskey didn't want Dr. No on the team plane. At least that's what McCaskey said. We all knew different. It might have been *his* team, but it was *my* sore ass. McCaskey wound up looking foolish for being so stubborn. And to think, if he'd have just let Hiroshi come with us, nobody would have known anything. There wouldn't have been a word about it in the newspapers.

Finally, Hiroshi Shiriashi showed up at the Hilton on Wednesday. He was accompanied by Bill Anderson of the Illinois Acupuncture Association. Anderson, who knew a good publicity opportunity when he saw one, was wearing some weird button on the lapel of his blue polyester suit. "Acupuncture Forever!" or something silly like that. I think Anderson took one too many needles in the head.

Whatever, we all went right to my room. I removed all my clothes, and Hiroshi went to work on my problem. I lay down, facedown, with my head sticking out from the foot of the bed so I could have a little chew of tobacco while Hiroshi did his thing. Becker, stretched out on the next bed, just shook his head. "All the nice-looking women in the world," he said. "And I gotta watch this."

Hiroshi, his eyes closed, was applying needle after needle to my left buttock. Thirty, forty needles to different points on my mosaic. Didn't hurt. No hassle. But, no noise, either. Early in the half-hour session, he had suddenly gotten up and pointed to the TV. Becker was watching a soap opera.

"Hiroshi requires complete quiet to perform," Anderson said, really businesslike.

Becker turned off the TV.

"What are you gonna do Sunday, Mac?" he said. "Have a Made in Japan label stamped on the back of your uniform?"

Steve Zucker, my attorney, who was sitting near the window, laughed. Anderson just glared. Ah, so. Hiroshi must have complete silence. Normally, I wouldn't let anybody stick anything into my rear end with his eyes closed, but, after all, this was the Super Bowl.

After the first go-round of needles, I got up and started running around the room, pretending I was a quarterback again. I felt better already. Because of my injury, I hadn't been able to move around at all. My mobility, going from side to side or planting my left foot to throw, was almost nil. But, just jumping around that room like a naked fool, I knew acupuncture was for me.

"Hiroshi," I said, "you're a genius."

"More," said Hiroshi, a man of few words.

I went down on the bed again for more needles. This went on, three or four treatments a day, right through Super Bowl morning. All the time, I felt better and better. After the Super Bowl, our trainer Fred Caito was quoted as saying that in the end, what saved me was the good old-fashioned pain-killer on the morning of the game. False. I did take a shot, but it wasn't Caito who made me healthy. It was Hiroshi.

That bothered Caito, obviously not a student of Oriental magic like me. He was totally opposed to acupuncture. Company man, Fred.

I had only one mix-up on appointments with Hiroshi. Becker and I, who had been out a couple nights before and were late for our first team meeting in New Orleans—Ditka threatened us with thousand-dollar fines if we did it again—decided to boogie on downtown again anyway. Dinner, beverages, a little music, more beverages.

I had told Hiroshi that I'd be back to my room at eleven o'clock Wednesday night, which was curfew. We missed it by a hair, and came strolling down the hall at around one-thirty in the morning. All of a sudden, I looked toward 5116 and there was this poor little Japanese guy hunched over in front of our door, like he was meditating. Must be a ritual for doctors of acupuncture.

"Beck," I said, "what the hell is he doing?"

"Waiting for your ass," he said. "It's late."

Hiroshi gave me another treatment, then went off to stay with Willie in his room. I knew I would be able to play Sunday. I was feeling good, in more ways than one.

That was, until Thursday morning. Early Thursday morning, when the phone rang. I picked it up. There was a lady on the other end.

"You rotten SOB!" she screamed. "How dare you say those things about us?"

Surely, I thought, I was having a nightmare. Then the phone rang again. It was a guy this time.

"You f—— a——!" he screamed. "Don't you show your face around this town anymore!"

By now, I knew something was up.

"What have you done now, Mac?" said Becker, still groggy.

"Nothing," I said. "Except the last two people who called here want to lynch me."

I didn't know what to make of it, so I got dressed and

went downstairs for our meeting and breakfast. Then, I started to get wind of what was happening. I ran into McCaskey, and he gave me the evil eye. Then along came Vainisi.

"Well, you've done it now, Jim," he said. "Did you say those things?"

"What things?" I said. Vainisi brushed me off. He didn't believe me. He was all bent out of shape anyway. He was sweating bullets, and he was dressed like he'd come over from the Salvation Army. He had on a grungy golf shirt and rumpled pants that looked like they hadn't been pressed since Super Bowl I. Later, I found out that he was so upset that he'd rifled through his bag of dirty laundry and rushed downstairs himself to find out about the things I'd said that I didn't say.

"You didn't say those things?" asked Ditka, whom I encountered next. I said I didn't know what he was talking about.

"Okay, Jim, I believe you," Ditka said. "We'll straighten this out."

Straighten what out? Would somebody please tell me what I didn't do?

Finally, Zucker got ahold of me and explained the non-story. Apparently, a New Orleans sportscaster had gone on the air Wednesday night with a report that I'd called all the town's women "sluts" and all the men "idiots." The guy's name is Buddy Diliberto. To this day, I couldn't pick him out of a crowd. I did see a picture of him in the newspaper and can tell you honestly he's not just another pretty face.

Naturally, my alleged remarks created an unbelievable uproar. The switchboards at the Bears' offices in the hotel were jammed with calls. The Hilton was getting bomb threats; some of our players were getting death threats. The people of New Orleans were furious, and I didn't blame them. But I was furious, too, because I never said what Buddy Boy said I said.

Pretty soon, the rumor unraveled. A radio station from Chicago, WLS, was doing its morning show from a restaurant in New Orleans called Toney's Spaghetti House. Supposedly, I was there at six o'clock Wednesday morning, all drunk and unruly. That's when I said what I didn't say. A local disc jockey who was also in the restaurant heard me say what I didn't say and later in the day talked with Buddy Diliberto.

Diliberto, like a boob, ran with it on the ten o'clock news. Now that's what I call responsible journalism: a hack—who people tell me talks like he's got a cork in his mouth—ending his sportscast with a report that a local disc jockey heard me call the women of New Orleans "sluts" over a Chicago radio show that had me on as a guest at six in the morning. All thirdhand "information." The guy never checked out anything. No facts. Just fiction. And then the media wonders why I'm skeptical and suspicious of the way it operates.

First of all, I was in bed at six Wednesday morning. In fact, I was in bed at nine Tuesday night because Becker and I were still hanging from the night before. Secondly, I do a lot of whacky things, but I don't ever remember eating spaghetti, or even wanting spaghetti, at six in the morning. That didn't stop people from believing it, though, because I'm me: crazy; wild; rude—you know, the whole bit.

Only one person believed me in the Bears' front office. Ditka, which I thought was cool. And the players knew the story was too bizarre, even for me. Not that they didn't pounce on it.

"I'm not standing next to *you* during the National Anthem Sunday," said Jay Hilgenberg, our center. "I don't want to get assassinated."

"I'm changing rooms," said Becker. Naturally, with my luck, there was another press conference scheduled for Thursday morning. The police were sweeping the hotel for explosives, there was a women's protest demonstration scheduled for the front of the hotel at noon, and I had to go meet my friends, the reporters. Ken Valdiserri and Bryan Harlan, the Bears' public relations directors, came to my room and told me I had to go down and face the music. I had to give my denial. I said, hell with it. I've had enough with all this crap. I had tried to be cooperative all week with them, and then I get stabbed in the back. I can get in enough trouble on my own. I don't need to be getting in trouble when I'm fast asleep. I called Nancy back in Chicago and warned her not to believe anything she heard on the radio or read in the papers. I was innocent.

Fortunately, the truth was starting to come out. Officials from the NFL, who were concerned, called the TV channel, WDSU, asking if anybody had proof of Diliberto's big scoop. Apparently, the general manager of the station was feeling the heat, too. He called Diliberto's actions "atrocious" and called Buddy Boy at home for a full explanation. They tell me Diliberto started to babble. They also tell me Diliberto is pretty good at babbling even when he's not broadcasting lies.

Zucker was keeping a cool head, as usual. He also believed my side. He knew I was in bed at nine Tuesday night. He was confident we could prove that Diliberto's pipe dream was a complete phony.

"Whether we can convince people that you went to sleep at a decent hour, I don't know," Zucker said. Then he popped the big one.

"Jim," he said, "you should go down to the press conference."

I wasn't thrilled by the idea, but I went, and it was mobbed. I told them the truth, that I couldn't remember the last time I ate spaghetti, that I never went on a Chicago radio show, that I never said anything about "sluts" or "idiots," and that, as a matter of fact, I kind of enjoyed the people and city of New Orleans. I could sense an air of disappointment. I was pretty convincing, I guess, and ninety-five percent of the reporters in that ballroom were hoping I was guilty. They wanted to hang me one more time.

"Jim's certainly taken the pressure off the rest of our players, hasn't he?" said Ditka.

Then, more retractions came in. The general manager of the TV station ordered Diliberto to rush downtown to the studio and apologize for being so stupid. I didn't see it, but the general manager led off the noon newscast with an apology to the Bears, the city of New Orleans, and me. Then Buddy Boy got his fat face on the air and did the same thing. Just begged to be forgiven; no scores and highlights today, folks.

Meanwhile, I got some help from an unexpected source. Les Grobstein, the sportscaster for WLS, made an appearance at the press conference. He was in New Orleans doing live reports back to Chicago. He came right out and said that he was at the restaurant Wednesday doing his early-morning shows and that I was nowhere in the area. He said Buddy Diliberto was a jerk.

That was nice to hear because Grobstein has called me a jerk, too, on occasion. We've had our moments in the past. But there he was, dressed up like an unmade bed, defending me in a crowded ballroom at the New Orleans Hilton. When I saw a hundred other media people interviewing Les Grobstein, I knew that Super Bowl week had slipped into the twilight zone. Not only did I make Buddy Diliberto famous, but Les Grobstein, too. Why me? Let me out of here.

Thank God, everything quieted down in a hurry. There were no bombs in the hotel. I thanked Ditka for trusting me and went over to practice, where at least my behind was feeling better all the time. I was ready to start throwing.

I still don't know if Jerry Vainisi got his laundry done. From the looks of him that crazy morning, I sure hope he did. As for Buddy Diliberto, the voice of reason and common sense in the great city of New Orleans, he was suspended for a couple weeks. He missed the Super Bowl, then returned to his job, telling it like it isn't.

I'm sorry to report that, to this day, I wouldn't know Buddy Diliberto if he came to my front door. I'm also sorry to report that he hasn't.

THREE

Headbands and Head Cases

"PLUTO."

Contrary to what a lot of people might think, that's not the planet where I was born. That's what I call my best friend, Dan Plater, who played football with me at Brigham Young, damn near died from an illness, but now is studying to be a doctor in California.

I felt like saying hello to Pluto, giving him a little publicity, so I wore his name on a headband during the Super Bowl. PLUTO. In big black letters on a white headband. That's one of the first questions I fielded after we abused the Patriots 46–10. Never mind all those points, all those yards. What's Pluto? Who's Pluto? Why Pluto?

Yeah, besides my sore behind and Buddy Boy Diliberto, that was the other big deal at the Super Bowl. Headbands. And, like all the other big deals, I couldn't conceive why there was so much commotion and controversy.

"What are you going to wear Sunday?"

I must have been asked that a thousand times, by reporters, by fans on the street, even by my teammates. I never dreamed headbands would become such a rage, but then, I don't totally understand people. People probably don't totally understand me, but I'm in the same boat with them.

Imagine people wearing headbands to walk around the block? To go to the grocery store? Am I responsible for that, too? I only wear a headband when I'm playing football. I'd never wear one to take a dog out in the morning, even if I owned a dog. But that's human nature. Fans grab on to something, and they jump all over it.

I wore a headband throughout college. It keeps perspiration from getting in your eyes, and it cuts down on your forehead becoming irritated by the helmet rubbing against it. No big deal. At least it wasn't until we played the Giants in our opening playoff game.

I'd signed on with Adidas, the athletic-equipment manufacturer, four years ago, and they had supplied me with blank headbands since. Then, starting with the Washington game in September—the Bears' fourth regular season game—they came out with a headband that had their name spelled across it. Simple. I wore them the rest of the season.

But then came the playoffs, and we started to get more attention than ever. When I took off my helmet on the sidelines—which I usually do—there wasn't *one* TV camera around. It seemed like there were *six*. They were all over Soldier Field for that game against the Giants. You were afraid to pick your nose for fear that you'd be on network television. Plus, this was my first postseason game in a Bears' uniform. I wanted it to go well.

I'd been warned before, through the Bears, that I was violating the uniform code. The party line was that advertisers pay millions of dollars for commercials during NFL telecasts, and it wasn't fair to them for me or any other player to give free advertising to any company that hired us to endorse their products.

I never gave it much thought, until after the Giant game.

We went to Suwanee, Georgia—the training complex used by the Atlanta Falcons—to practice in better weather for our next game, the NFC Championship back in Chicago against Los Angeles. We had a team meeting and one of the topics Ditka brought up caught my attention.

"Jim McMahon," he said, "has been fined five thousand dollars by the NFL for wearing the Adidas headband last week against New York."

It didn't take me long to form an opinion.

"I ain't paying it," I said.

I never did. Actually, the NFL had fined the Bears, who passed it on to me. I haven't paid it yet. I never heard any complaints from Adidas. Pretty good publicity for them, don't you think?

Still, I didn't know what to do about headbands for our next game. I didn't want to keep running up fines, even if I wasn't going to pay them, but I didn't want to give in to a rule that made no sense. What about all the players who wear helmets with a brand name right in front? They don't paint over that name. You see it all the time on TV when they zoom in on a guy. What's the difference? Does the NFL get a slice of the action from those companies? I don't know, but it does seem to create a double standard, doesn't it?

Anyway, before the Rams game, I still hadn't decided what to do. We took the pregame warm-up—I was wearing my Adidas headband—and I came inside to the locker room. Michael McCaskey walked over to my locker and warned me again. He said it would just make more trouble if I wore the Adidas headband again.

"Why don't you wear one that says 'Space for Rent'?" he suggested. "Why not 'Halas'?"

Well, I wasn't about to wear one for Halas. When I was drafted by the Bears, he didn't exactly roll out the red carpet for me. Besides, we already had his initials on our shirt-sleeves, GSH. No, not Halas. Sorry, Mr. President.

Then McCaskey came up with another idea. Why not put

"Rozelle" on there for Pete Rozelle, the NFL commissioner who'd fined me? He was going to be in the press box that day. Good move, I thought. Why not give Pete a little publicity? Maybe that would get him off my back.

So, there I was, minutes before the NFC Championship, taking a bunch of blank headbands and writing "Rozelle" on them with a felt-tip pen. The other players thought I was nuts, which meant they hadn't changed their minds about me since the regular season.

While I was busy doing my artwork, Wally, who dressed near me, came over.

"Make me one up, too, Mac," Payton said. So I drew *him* one with "Rozelle" on it. He also worked for a firm, also wore its headband, and also was annoyed by the league's nit-picking.

The TV cameras had a ball. They took a bunch of shots during the game of the "Rozelle" headbands. Even the commissioner got a laugh out of it. He saw the whole thing from his seat in the press box, and on the TV monitors, and he took it all well. He even sent me a handwritten note on his own stationery, right when he got back to New York:

Jan. 13, 1986

Dear Jim,

I was really upset yesterday with your headband because:

1—I didn't have my shoe model ready to sell so the promotion was useless.

2—I lost a little of what's left of my personal privacy.

It was funny as hell!!

You and your 'friends' have done a tremendous job on the field and captivated the entire country.

Look forward to seeing you in New Orleans.

Regards,
Pete

I thought that was nice of him, even if he didn't mention anything about forgetting the $5,000 fine.

Naturally, the newspapers and sportscasts pounced on the headband issue. There were pictures of me and my "Rozelle" creation all over, and when we arrived in New Orleans, the stores were selling "Rozelle" headbands with all the other Super Bowl souvenirs. Some for $4.95; some for $3.95. Crazy. There were also headbands with "McMahon" written on them and all different things. There was even a headband made up by a really creative person. It read, "Headband."

Along with all the threatening phone calls from the Buddy Boy incident, I got a lot of headbands sent to me in New Orleans. A bunch of them were mailed to the hotel. There were others simply addressed to "Jim McMahon, c/o Superdome." Fur headbands, a headband that lit up, headbands with people's names on them. Imagine that. Complete strangers wanted me to wear their headbands in front of a hundred million viewers on Super Bowl Sunday.

Obviously, I had to make some serious decisions about my game-day wardrobe. I thought about wearing one that said "Alvin." That's Rozelle's real first name, one he doesn't like to be called by, apparently. I backed off that. I might get fined $50,000, and the next note he sent me might not have been so cheerful. Buddy Ryan, our defensive coordinator, was leaving the Bears after the Super Bowl, or so many of us thought. I thought about wearing one for him. I also thought about wearing another "Buddy," for Diliberto. Maybe "Buddy . . . Get a Job." But I'd already made him famous. Screw him.

What else? I thought. I'd been on *Late Night with David Letterman*, and he gave me a headband during the show. Maybe one with "Hiroshi" for my favorite acupuncturist? While I was in New Orleans, *Rolling Stone* magazine sent a reporter to spend a few days with me for a cover story. I'd always wanted to be on the cover of *Rolling Stone*. They also sent along a headband. It went on and on. I had hundreds.

"What about wearing one for Juvenile Diabetes?" suggested Zucker, whose son, Herbie, is diabetic.

I liked that idea a lot. Why not put some charities up there? Also while I was in New Orleans, I got a letter from someone about all the American soldiers still missing in Vietnam since the war. Then he followed up with a couple phone calls. He said I could really help the cause. Another good idea.

My teammates were asking me about what I had in mind. You could tell they were really getting nervous about the Super Bowl. We had to beat the New England Patriots or the media would have hung us. So, what were the guys talking about? My headbands. I told you this team was demented.

Gary Haeger, who helps to keep track of our equipment, was in charge of my headbands. I gave him a few to hang on to on the sidelines, and then I changed after every couple series or so.

The "JDF-CURE" headband went over well. I wore that early in the game. Zucker told me the Juvenile Diabetes Foundation was swamped with donations for weeks after the Super Bowl. When I went to Hawaii for the Pro Bowl the next week, there was a knock at the door one day. We opened, and there was this huge arrangement of flowers and balloons that JDF had sent Nancy and me as thanks. The "POW-MIA" also got a good response. An organization of Illinois Vietnam veterans gave me an award. I appreciated that. I don't think I would have been too good at war. I'm glad I was born when I was. If I'd have had to go to Vietnam, I would have been one of those guys who lose it and play Russian roulette.

I also wore one urging support for children's hospitals and one for United Way, which is the official charity of the NFL. I thought that might be good for some brownie points with Alvin. I mean Pete.

The headband that meant the most to me, though, was the one for "Pluto." Now, there's another charity case. Actually, he's done great things with his life, and I love him like a brother, just like I always have, from the first time I met him at Brigham Young. I was a sophomore, and he was this skinny freshman from Reno, Nevada, always laughing and joking.

Dan was a Mormon, like most of the other students at BYU—not me, not on your life. But the difference was, Pluto was normal. He liked to have a few beverages and mess around. We became fast friends and even lived together for one hellacious summer out there.

Pluto was also a damn good wide receiver. The last three seasons at BYU, he caught 123 passes for 1,962 yards and 16 touchdowns. He could have made the Bears when he got out of school; I know that. Instead, he was drafted by the Denver Broncos, who didn't really give him a chance. Then, he went to the Cincinnati Bengals during the strike year of 1982, when everybody missed seven weeks of the season because we were fighting our usual losing battle with owners.

The next year, my second in Chicago, I got Pluto a tryout with the Bears. He came to live with Nancy and me in June, and we were having a great old time. When we weren't playing football, we were playing golf. Preferably, the latter. And when we couldn't do either, we usually could be found having a few cocktails somewhere. I was happy to be around my best friend again, and I felt sure he'd make the team.

Right around mini-camp, though, Pluto started complaining about having headaches all the time. He was also saying that he had trouble seeing, that he couldn't pick out objects that were right in front of his face. You wouldn't have known it in camp, because he was catching the ball fine, but he was worried. And it wasn't like Pluto to worry too much.

"I must have a friggin' brain tumor or something," he said to me one day. I didn't know how to take that, but, being interested in medicine and pointed toward a career as a doctor one day, Pluto had an idea.

It finally got so bad that Pluto went to the eye doctor, who told him he couldn't be of any help. Couldn't figure out what the problem was. So, then Pluto went to a neurosurgeon and the news wasn't good. Pluto did have a brain tumor. They operated right away, opened him up ear to ear. They couldn't get it all, so they went in again right away, through his nose, and got most of it. The doctors told his wife, Adrian, that they didn't know whether Pluto was going to live and, if he did, whether he'd ever be able to see again. They didn't know whether he was too far gone and didn't know whether the pressure on the optic nerve had ruined his eyes forever. Most of the other people who had what he had were either dead or blind.

Thank God, Pluto came out of it all right by some miracle. And fortunately, he had something to fall back on. He went to medical school at USC, where he finished something like third in a class of 150 during his second year. That wasn't surprising, because Pluto always applied himself. We had a lot in common. Always slapping each other around, always raising hell, always wrestling and laughing about something. The big difference was, Pluto was conscientious. He hit the books. I watched my books get dusty.

To this day, Pluto and I talk all the time. He misses football, I'm sure, and I know he wished he could have been there with us in New Orleans. The next best thing, I thought, was to remember him Super Bowl Sunday, let him know I was thinking of him.

When I got back to the hotel after the game, the first phone call I made was to Pluto in California.

"Did you see it? Did you see the headband?" I said.

"Mac, you're too sweet," he said. "Thanks, buddy."

I wish I could say that the headband issue went as smoothly. I did run into Rozelle at the Pro Bowl a few days later, and we joked some more about the whole thing. He said he was upset now about not getting a commission on all those headbands that had his name on them. He wanted at least a ten percent cut, maybe twenty-five. We got along well, I thought, though I'm not about to get too chummy with the commissioner.

Besides, the NFL decided to become even tougher with the uniform rule during the off-season. They were talking about a stiffer penalty for anyone who violated policy, a penalty like throwing the player out of a game. Throwing a player out of a game for wearing a headband? And you don't need to be told who thought up the proposal, do you? Why, the Bears, of course.

Michael McCaskey, our peerless leader, had no choice during the 1985 season, because we were 18–1 and not about to be pushed around. But, if he had his choice, he'd have forty-five players with no personality, no individuality at all. Michael McCaskey would like a bunch of robots. Then, everything would go along peacefully. You might not win many games, but at least there wouldn't be any headbands. Logical, right?

I don't know what it is about the Bears and the NFL. Players are entertainers. This is an entertainment business. Why take the fun out of it? Why does everything have to be so dull, so serious? Did I really hurt anybody by wearing headbands with Adidas on them? I might have helped some people with the others I wore. But, do they think of that?

Steve Zucker, my agent-adviser, was furious when all this hit the fan a couple months after the Super Bowl, at the NFL owners meeting. He talked about a lawsuit of some sort, and I'm not sure where this thing will end up. I know we aren't planning to give in.

I also know the Bears were getting a little testy about us telling our side of the story. When they put the Super Bowl trophy on display in downtown Chicago, Michael McCaskey looked over at Zucker and said, very sarcastically, something about how he was "Mister Freedom of Speech." It's a good thing I wasn't there, or else I'd have painted a few words on McCaskey's forehead. Not "Rozelle," either.

Players wear different gloves, different shoes, different

everything, from all sorts of companies. Whenever you look out on the field, you see logos. What's the problem? And if fans identify with what I did, kind of a good-natured jab at the Establishment, that isn't all bad, either. It was good for a few laughs. Sometimes in the NFL, you get the idea that's against the law.

I infuriated a few people in the front office with my headbands, but if I helped make one dollar for charity, and if I made my best buddy Pluto happy, that's all that mattered. Plus, I got in a last lick at the NFL and Bears, at least for last season.

I didn't wear an Adidas headband during the Super Bowl around my head, but I did wear it around my neck. They'll make that illegal, too, of course, but they're too late. I stick-handled around that bit of legislation. Some rules are just too silly not to be bent or broken. Touché.

F O U R

The Coach and Me

I've heard it said many times that a good team is the team that reflects the personality of its coach. That theory certainly applied to the 1985 Chicago Bears. Mike Ditka can't stand losing. We couldn't stand losing.

A lot of people probably think I can't stand Ditka, either, but that isn't entirely true. I totally respect his attitude about wanting to win, about doing anything to win, and not worrying about all the nickel-dime things that some other coaches waste time on.

We've had our moments, and I'm sure we probably will as long as he's the boss and I'm his quarterback. He says I do certain things for the sole purpose of aggravating him. I really don't. I really don't wake up every morning wondering, "How can I annoy Ditka today?" It's hard enough just to wake up in the morning, let alone think and plot.

There was a period last season when I was hurt, and we didn't talk for a few weeks. Never exchanged a civil word.

Jerry Vainisi even called me up to his office one day after practice, sat me down, and told me I had to resolve this personality conflict with Mike. Personality conflict? What personality conflict? I was injured. I wasn't playing. There was no reason for him to talk to me, or for me to talk to him.

Besides, it wasn't all that true, as Ditka pointed out when he was asked about the situation. He said he had talked to me during that time when we weren't talking. He came over to me on the sidelines in Dallas and screamed at me, "Shut the ——— up, McMahon!" That's talking, isn't it? And I know it was Mike, because his veins were sticking out of his neck and his face was red as a beet, like it was ready to explode. That had to be my good friend Sybil, the one who wears a necktie on the sidelines, the one we all figure will strangle himself someday with the same necktie. He'll get mad, and he'll reach to make that knot tighter, and by the time the paramedics get to him with the oxygen, it'll be too late. I'll have to take over as head coach.

Anyway, I remember clearly why that happened in Dallas. That was the game when we humiliated the Cowboys 44–0. Steve Fuller started for us at quarterback, and did a great job. Our defense was awesome, as usual. Anyway, I was yelling along our bench for our guys to really give it to the Dallas quarterback, Danny White, which they eventually did.

"Shut the ——— up, McMahon!" Ditka roared.

"What's the problem, Mike?" I asked.

"They get Danny White hurt, and they'll put in [Gary] Hogeboom, and he's better than White," Ditka said. "So shut up."

Oh.

I just walked away from him. That was the same day he got mad at me because of the way I was dressed. I had on a normal shirt and blue jeans. Faded blue jeans. I mean, aren't blue jeans supposed to be faded? He got mad because he thought I didn't look presentable. Hell, I had a pair of ostrich boots on that were worth more than his whole wardrobe. Like I said, Mike doesn't worry about the unimportant things. Most of the time, anyway.

We had another episode later in the season at Giants Stadium against the New York Jets. I called an audible and Walter Payton just got smashed on the play, sort of like when I screwed up early in the Super Bowl. When I got back to the sidelines, I could see that Mike wasn't in the best of moods. I don't know how I was able to make that deduction. Maybe it was the fact that, with sixty thousand people screaming in the arena, Mike's voice was the only one anybody heard.

"You c——, you mother——," he yelled at me.

"——— you," I said.

The national TV cameras recorded our little conversation. That was a Saturday in December. The next day, with a lot of other pro football on, the people from CBS asked me to stay over in New York to appear on the *NFL Today* show.

Naturally, they had those film clips ready, and naturally, they asked me about the incident.

"Well," I said, "that about sums up our relationship." I never lie, particularly on Sundays.

But, Mike Ditka has mellowed since we both came to the Bears in 1982. He was really uptight when he started as coach. One of the worst things he did was get all over guys for making mistakes. Taking them out of games, screaming at them in public, going crazy on the sidelines. It got so that players couldn't relax, they were so afraid of what Ditka might do if they dropped a pass or missed an assignment. He could really be out of control, so badly that he'd lose a grasp on the game itself. He was the Monster of the Midway.

Ditka was just as hard on himself. We'd heard stories about some of the wild things he did as an assistant with the Cowboys before he left Dallas for Chicago. He could throw a pretty mean clipboard, we were told. He could throw a pretty good fit, too. A major-league temper, Mike Ditka had.

We found that out after our fourth game of the 1983 season,

which we lost in overtime at Baltimore 22–19. Ditka came into the locker room and started pounding at an equipment locker. All of a sudden he looked up at the trainer and said, "I think I broke my hand." He had. We didn't know whether to laugh or cry.

During the last couple years, Ditka hasn't been quite as high-strung, and that helped the players play better. I'm sure the fact that we were 18–1 meant that he let us get away with some things that we never would have gotten away with otherwise, but the point is, Ditka was most concerned about how we played on Sunday. He didn't bug us about some of the nutty things we said or did.

Of course, he did and said some pretty strange things himself. There was that sixth game of 1985, when we whipped the 49ers in San Francisco 26–10. That not only kept us unbeaten at 6–0; it repaid the 49ers for knocking us out of the playoffs the year before. Mike really wanted to win that game. Something awful. And he told us if we did, he had some real special wine that he'd share with us on the long flight back to Chicago that night.

Well, we never got to taste any of that wine. And when Mike took one walk to the back of the plane from where he was sitting in front, the players found out why. Mike had tasted all of the wine himself. He was smashed, hammered, bobbing, weaving. There's no way he should have been allowed to drive home that night. Apparently, he was offered a lift by Vainisi and a few others who felt the same way. Apparently, the police felt the same way, too.

Five minutes after we left O'Hare Airport, he was pulled over for drunk driving. He had said something on TV from San Francisco after the game about how he might celebrate a little on the plane coming back, and how he might not be able to even see when he got back home. Evidently, the Illinois State Police were watching.

A few of us take the same highway to our houses that he

uses, and he damn near ran over a couple guys. Ditka was all over the road. He'd have killed himself if he hadn't gotten stopped by the cops. A few miles down the road, when we caught up to where he'd been nailed, we saw his car on the side with the police car. Nobody pulled over. We just honked our horns, and drove on by. I guess his wife, Diana, had to come and get him.

The next morning, I heard about it on the radio on the way to Halas Hall. So had most of the other guys. Naturally it was a hot topic in the locker room, and then Mike held his meeting. He didn't look too good. He looked like a coach who hadn't lost a game but had lost his license for a few months.

"Fellas . . . I did something very stupid last night," said Ditka. There were a few of us in that room coughing real loud to keep from breaking up. That must have been real special wine indeed.

That's one of the things that bothers me about Ditka, who was a mean and rough tight end for the Bears when they won the NFL title in 1963. He was a hell-raiser as a player. They tell this story about George Halas showing films one day when he was still coach. He was pointing out some things about the next opponent—strengths, weaknesses, that sort of thing. All of a sudden, Mike got up in the back of the room and yelled at the top of his lungs, "F—— 'em!" I don't know if the story is true, but it sure sounds like Ditka.

So does that anecdote about how Ditka was fighting with Halas, trying to get a raise. Ditka got angry and frustrated and said, "The Old Man throws quarters around like manhole covers." Way to go, Mike! That's what I mean when I say Ditka probably would have been a great guy to have as a teammate, a lot more fun than he is to have as a coach. We'd have probably been out drinking every night. I know *he* would have been out every night. I know *I* would have been out drinking every night. Only stands to reason that we would have gone out *together* every night. As it is, now that he's a coach, Mike has changed a little bit. The same team he left because of a contract problem, the Bears, is the team that pays his check now, a pretty good check. While he was an assistant coach in Dallas, Ditka wrote a letter of application for the Bears' head coaching job to the same man he fought with, Halas. Now, Ditka's all loyal to the Bears again.

Also, this guy who could do the streets at night with the best of them is now telling my roommate, Kurt Becker, and me to watch ourselves. I had a bad first half in Tampa last year, and he came over babbling something about, "That's what you get for staying out all night." I hadn't been out all night, not even half a night, but that's Mike.

Ditka also told Becker to warn me that alcohol and football don't mix. He told Becker that he would fine us one week's paycheck if we got caught breaking curfew. He told Becker that the management might have to put a cage around our room on the road just to keep us in at night. This is from a coach who gets picked up by the police for driving under the influence! That never happened to me. Besides, I don't mix my alcohol with football anyway. I don't mix my alcohol with anything. I prefer beer. Much better for you than wine.

If it sounds like I'm saying Mike is a hypocrite, I'm really not. He just does some weird things. He's a born-again Christian who says he's very religious, which is fine. But I guess for three hours every Sunday that doesn't hold, because some of the words that come out of his mouth when he's coaching, *I* wouldn't even use. Some of the words, I never even heard!

But it all goes back to the purpose, I guess, and that is, Mike Ditka just wants to win. Wants to win more than anything. Every so often, he gives you that same line: If you forty-five guys don't want to play, we'll go out and get forty-five guys who do. That's part of his prima-donna speech. You know, you guys are all prima donnas. When you hear that twice a week, it tends to get old. Mike has to get some new material.

Still, he's great at keeping players levelheaded. He has to know that, with the 1985 Bears, there weren't a whole lot of attitude problems. Just like he had to know that we weren't a bunch of prima donnas. We worked our butts off, and he knew it. But whether he wanted us to know he knew is another matter. He was forever reviewing films of Sunday victories on Monday and knocking us down to size.

We finished our regular season, for instance, in Detroit. We beat the Lions 37–17 to finish 15–1. It wasn't a great performance, and we realized that, but it got the job done. Then Ditka got rolling after the game and told us we were horsefeathers, that we had no chance in the playoffs if we continued to play that way. Here we had just won a game on the road by 20 to go 15–1, and he's giving us grief.

"You've got a couple days off for Christmas, fellas," he said. "I hope you go home and find yourselves."

On the flight home that night—it was a short one, so we didn't have any special wine on board—I slipped up front and grabbed hold of the public-address system. I told the guys that we were about to land, that they should have a happy holiday, but above all, they should try to find themselves. (I knew where I'd find myself for the holidays. Right near the beverages.) When I walked to the back of the plane, the guys were roaring. I never did look at Ditka, but I don't imagine he found anything funny in my sick and sarcastic humor.

I do think, though, that down deep Ditka respects a guy who will stand up for what he believes. He might even like me for that, in some strange way, because that's the way he is. Mike doesn't watch every word he says. He's not afraid to say something that's going to motivate the next week's opponent, because he knows next week's game is going to be won on the field, not in the newspapers. You against us, baby. Let's see who's better. Let's see who's stronger. That's the way Mike operates. That's the way I think.

Considering his background as a bona fide free spirit, I

don't think Mike can expect us all to be the same, on the field or off. He knows that you can't have forty-five guys locking themselves in their rooms at eight o'clock the night before a game. Some guys will, which is fine. I can't. For one thing, I can't sleep that well or that long before a game. I like to go out and have a few beverages and relax. Sometimes, I forget to check the clock, but it's ridiculous to be knocking on doors of grown men, making sure they don't break curfew. Fortunately, Mike isn't into that. Every once in a while he'll give you a little message, to let you know that he's watching. But, when you win, like we won, a good coach is going to let a lot slide.

Is Mike Ditka a good coach? Well, he knows the game, but he gets a little wrapped up in his innovations sometimes. That's surprising, because he is a basic guy, no frills. Like I said, you and me and let's see who's better. But he did spend a lot of time in Dallas under Tom Landry, the head coach of the Cowboys, and Mike gets caught up with all those different formations and a lot of movement. That's great stuff, if you know what you're doing. Thing is, the more complex you make the game, the more chances you have of mistakes. If it were up to me, football would be as simple as possible. Mike is that way, down deep, but every once in a while, when he gets his thinking cap on, you never know quite what to expect.

He can be very stubborn, too. I've talked to his assistant coaches, and they say he's a good guy to work for. He listens, he can have some fun, and he doesn't demand that you spend twenty-four hours a day on the job, looking at films and all that—even though Mike is a real worker, in his office at 5:00 A.M. during the season. I don't know when he sees his family. They also tell me Mike's pretty good at taking a game plan that's been carefully drawn up by the staff, then changing it all around, to do it his way. After we went 18–1, Mike Ditka probably thinks he's a genius.

Maybe he is, in a way. Not with the *X*'s and *O*'s, but in getting players committed to win. When I first got to the Bears, the attitude wasn't very good. He said there were too many guys around whose highlight of the week wasn't game day, but payday. You don't want to pay the price, he said, you guys who are just putting in time and going through the motions.

I'll give Ditka full credit for getting rid of them. He wanted no part of them, and he let them know, and he gave them a chance to do it his way. When they didn't they were gone. That's what got this ball rolling, the selection of the right forty-five guys. Mike was right when he said that some of our so-called second- or third-stringers might not have the ability of a lot of other players on teams that didn't win the Super Bowl. But our guys were perfect for us; they fit in just right.

Mike, as committed as he is to God, doesn't believe it's God's will when you lose a game. There was a lot of that on the Bears a few years ago, too. We had a few players who would pray in the shower room, all by themselves. These are the same guys who might drop a pass and say, "Well, He meant it that way." Well, I believe in God, and I believe that God's will is that everybody tries his hardest, everybody tries to succeed, to win. You can use God as an inspiration, but not as a crutch.

That was just one of the factions, or cliques, that used to hurt the Bears. I mean, when you have a few guys going off by themselves to pray before a game, it sort of sets them apart. A lot of people would have trouble believing this, but I say a little prayer to God before every game, too. I ask him to help me do my best, to help me to stay healthy for my family's sake. But I don't run off and do it away from my teammates. And if I play a lousy game, I don't say it was the Lord's will.

I'm partial, of course. I think if you have forty-five beer-drinking fools who love each other, you've got a good chance of having a good football team. Judging by some of the things Mike's done as coach, I have to think he partly agrees. We don't have the divisions in the team we used to have. We don't have the offense on one side of the room and the defense on another side, blaming each other. We're all together, and Ditka is a big reason for that. He kept stressing that you can't be pointing fingers, that it's not the offensive team or the defensive team that matters. It's the team, period. The Bears.

Ditka can get under your skin at times, that's for sure. He'll get you just furious enough at him that you'll go out and knock a guy's block off, just to get him off your back, just to prove him wrong. Ditka's pretty smart that way. He keeps pushing and pushing until you're right at the edge. But then, he also knows when to lift you up. He's a man's man, when you get right down to it. The way he stuck up for me during Super Bowl week, when that fool of a sportscaster in New Orleans spread false rumors, well, that shows a lot about Ditka.

And, serious as he is, Mike can make you laugh. He can make some real strong pregame speeches, but he can also go the other way. The Saturday night before the Super Bowl, he showed up for our meeting and it was obvious he wasn't going to give us the "Win one for the Gipper" business. Instead, he started mocking some of the bizarre things that had taken place all week, especially involving me.

He was wearing sunglasses; he brought up the headbands, and the acupuncture; and then he turned around and dropped his pants right in our faces. That was his way of toasting my sore behind, I suppose. That was also his way of mimicking what I'd done earlier that week, when a helicopter flew over our secret practice session. I flipped 'em a moon, just to show everybody where I hurt. Mike was just trying to act as demented as me. It worked. It was pretty funny.

They say that there's a lot of Mike Ditka in me, and a lot of me in Mike Ditka. That might be true. Some of the things he does make me mad and some of the things I do make him mad. But, we both want to do the same thing: win and let the rest take care of itself. If I had a dime, I'd still call him if I was in trouble, if I needed help. I'd want him on my side in a fight, too. And, like I said, if we were teammates, I'm sure we'd go out for a few beers often—unless, of course, he wanted to drink wine. In that case, I'd make sure to drive him home.

FIVE

The Kremlin's Team

Around the NFL, the Dallas Cowboys have been known for several years as "America's Team." You know, successful, clean-cut, God-fearing, and all that. A nice image for the country's youth, because they had all those wonderful role models. The Cowboys ate up the idea, and, of course, so did just about everybody in Dallas.

So, when we went to Dallas and ate up the Cowboys 44–0 on November 17, 1985—a date I'll never forget because I hate the Cowboys—the natural question was, would the Chicago Bears replace Dallas as "America's Team"?

Dan Hampton thought it over for about three seconds in the locker room. "I don't know if we want to be 'America's Team,' " he said, pretty well speaking for all of us. "But, if we keep playing like we are, they might just start calling us 'The Kremlin's Team.' "

I've got no use for the Russians, but Hampton was right on. We were deranged and crazy and good and, on top of it all, we had fun. I can't imagine any team in football having as much fun as we had in 1985. I know what you're thinking. How can you win eighteen out of nineteen games plus the Super Bowl and not have fun? That's true. But, unlike a lot of other championship teams in the past, we were an unruly bunch of guys, a group of characters with characters.

Including Walter Payton. I've got a little secret for you. Payton isn't as serious as he's made out to be. He's one of the leading pranksters on the team. He's forever screwing around during meetings. And if he's got a few spare moments around Halas Hall, you might just hear him shooting off his pellet gun through the locker room.

Wally is without a doubt the greatest football player I've ever seen, and certainly the best I've ever played with. He's a fabulous athlete, with tremendous instincts, and if he weren't the all-time leading rusher in the NFL, I'm sure he'd be the all-time something else. He can catch the ball, he can block, he can punt, and he can throw. He's taken a few turns at quarterback during the years, and he's a natural. There isn't anything he can't do, except maybe keep a straight face all the time.

Maybe that's what keeps him going—his sense of humor, his playful ways, his realization that so much of the stuff around him is red tape. Don't forget, he played eleven years with the Bears before he won a Super Bowl. He's played on a lot of mediocre teams, and a lot of lousy teams, and because he didn't always get the kind of blocking our offensive line gave him in 1985, he took a lot of punishment.

And yet, the man's missed only one game in professional football because of injury. Of all his statistics, that's the most amazing one to me. He plays hurt, and he plays hard. It's been an honor to play with him, and like I said about the Super Bowl game, Wally can be a factor even when he's not gaining a lot of yards. Just the fact that he's there, on our side, means so much to the Bears.

Off the field, Wally seems a little mysterious, and he probably likes it that way. He keeps to himself pretty much. I don't see him much on the road. If he's going to go out for dinner with anybody, it'll probably be Matt Suhey, our veteran fullback. But that's fine. For a superstar, Wally is totally unselfish. I consider him a friend; I hope he considers me one.

Mike Singletary, our All-Pro middle linebacker, is another player I really admire. He's not all that big, but he's completely devoted, and works like a dog at his profession. When he isn't keeping himself in shape physically, he's staying late after practice to watch films. Or, he'll take home films of our next opponent and watch them there. I'd go absolutely bananas if I put as much time in as he does. I'd also be bored. But Buddy Ryan, who called Singletary all the rotten names in the book when he showed up as a rookie from Baylor, said it right. Buddy said Mike Singletary was the best football player he'd ever coached.

Mike is very religious, but I guarantee you that if he misses a tackle, which he hardly ever does, he doesn't blame it on God's will. Mike will even swear on occasion, though I've never seen him smoke or drink. Like I said, if I went through football that way, I'd be a basket case. A bored basket case. But my helmet's off to him. I'm glad Mike Singletary is on our side.

What's The Refrigerator really like? I can't tell you how many people ask me that question. William Perry became a folk hero during 1985; he also became a millionaire a couple times over, from what I hear. But it wouldn't have happened if he was a jerk. He's a good guy. How can you not like somebody who laughs at himself? Am I fat, like everyone says I am? Of course I'm fat, he says. And he is, though not as fat as when he first showed up for training camp. The first time I saw William I thought he would faint in the heat, and he almost did. He practiced once, and then he went right into the dehydration tank. But after he lost a few pounds, and started to play more, he got better. He learned. And then when he started scoring touchdowns, he became the most famous three-hundred-pounder in sports. Maybe anywhere in the world.

If anybody resented all the publicity The Fridge got, it would have been Suhey. When Perry came in on those short-yardage situations, he was taking Matt's place, and some of Matt's fanfare. But I think Suhey was like the rest of us. He just sat back, shook his head, and enjoyed this load having so much fun.

I liked The Fridge right away in training camp. He was on his own diet there, a real strict one of vegetables and fruit. Every so often, I'd be near him in line and tease him by throwing some chicken on his tray. He would probably have killed to eat it, but all he did was laugh. That was July. By January, he was laughing all the way to the bank. The Fridge didn't do all that much. He was a defensive tackle who didn't even make our starting lineup for a while. He might even be a better offensive lineman, because it would take a defensive end an hour to get around him. But Ditka created The Fridge, and The Fridge became a star. More power to him.

What can I say about Dan Hampton? John Hannah of the New England Patriots said it all at the Pro Bowl. Hannah said if you're a good football player, it doesn't matter where you line up, you'll get the job done. He was referring to Hampton, the perfect example of a guy who just loves to play. Dan is a big ol' country boy from Arkansas who likes to play the guitar and hear himself talk on occasion, but he is something else on Sundays.

Steve McMichael, also a defensive tackle, is more the strong and silent type, which might cost him when it comes to getting publicity. He should have been an All-Pro in 1985, but wasn't. That makes him the most underrated lineman in football. He had a lot to do with making us mean. The man plays hard every down, every day, even in practice. He works as hard as anybody, and harder than most. He works like every play will be his last, but he isn't much for being quoted, which is why he kids Hampton about being a prima donna. Steve will sit next to Dan after a game and just listen to Hampton ramble on. Then, if a reporter comes over to Steve, he'll repeat a lot of what Hampton said, just so Hampton can hear it.

You look at McMichael and you think he's totally off-the-wall, but he knows where he's going. He's different. He's like me. He doesn't give a damn what other people think about him. He just wants to go out there and punish people. Hampton said we played the 1985 season with more heart than any team in the NFL, and he's right. And McMichael was one of the reasons for that.

Jay Hilgenberg? What a story he is. They ought to make a movie about him. He came to the Bears as a rookie free agent out of Iowa in 1981. The Bears had a Monday night game in Detroit and lost 48–17, with the Lions' Eric Hipple throwing for four touchdowns. Hilgy was on the sidelines for that game, talking with Revie Sorey.

"Revie," he said. "We're probably the worst team in the league right now." Revie just listened.

"And since I'm the only player who didn't play for us tonight," Hilgy went on, "that means I must be the worst player in the league."

And now look at Jay Hilgenberg. He's the best center in the NFL. Dwight Stephenson of the Miami Dolphins, a veteran center, used to get most of the ink. But last year, Hilgy finally started to get his due. Which is only fair, because Hilgy has really worked to get where he is, even if he is lazy.

You say that doesn't make sense? The 1985 Chicago Bears weren't supposed to make sense. But we did make other teams miserable, and Richard Dent was right up front in that department. He was our defensive end, our Super Bowl Most Valuable Player. He led the league in sacking quarterbacks, even if he was earning only $90,000 from our wildly generous management.

As good as I think Richard is on Sundays, I enjoy him even more on Mondays, when I get to look at the films. During the game, when you're on the sidelines, you're busy getting ready for your next series on offense. So, you don't always fully appreciate what the defense is doing. That's where Mondays come in handy. That's when I realized how much time Richard Dent spent in the other teams' backfields. He is awesome.

Dent isn't much of a practice player. During the week, he'll loaf and line up offside and get all the coaches mad. But then on Sundays, he does some things during games that are unbelievable. He's got a bad body, an ugly body. Wally always kids him for being all legs and all ass. Wally pretends he's Dent and says he's going to get some money out of his wallet. Then he reaches over his shoulder, as if to say that's how high up on his body Dent's legs extend. But that's probably where Richard gets most of his power. For his size, he's got a tremendous first step, tremendous acceleration. Then he just keeps on going. He overpowers the guy trying to block him, then bores in on the quarterback with that wingspan of his. I don't know how many passes he deflected last year, but I do know that when he got to the quarterback, it was all over. Richard not only has the knack of hitting the passer, but he drives a guy into the ground. As a quarterback, I know that's what hurts most. Not the initial contact. You sort of brace for that. But when a guy decides he wants to screw you into the ground, it's not the ground that gives, especially if you're playing on artificial turf. It's your body. Richard Dent? I tell you, he's flat-out scary, bad body and all.

Willie Gault, on the other hand, is real pretty. He's our wide receiver, and I admit, we've had our moments. Football isn't the most important thing in Willie's life. He's a former Olympic hurdler and sprinter on his way to Hollywood, or so he hopes. He wants to be an actor. He's just stopping off in Chicago, playing his latest role as a football player.

I'll say this about Willie. He showed me something in the playoffs and Super Bowl. He made some big catches. In the past, I've felt he heard footsteps, that he didn't like getting into traffic. You can't depend on a guy like that. You have to know that a guy is going to run his route, even if the game isn't on national TV, even if there's a good chance of getting hit hard. Speed is great. I guess you have to have it. But if you can't depend on a guy, what good is it to have him outrunning everybody else if he doesn't run the right route? Good thing is, Willie's improving all the time.

Dennis McKinnon, on the other hand, is a tough guy, a worker, a receiver you can bank on, even if he's going for the ball with four defensive players on his back. Dennis is going to stick his nose in, and he's not going to back off. Dennis's problem is that he has bad knees, and in 1985, he came back too soon from knee surgery. Then he had to sit out, and he came back too soon again. He played in pain all year, and then, after the Super Bowl, the doctors said he was so messed up he'd have to miss the entire 1986 season. That would be no way for us to defend a Super Bowl title, without McKinnon. I have a feeling Dennis will ask for a second opinion. He comes to play, and so does another of our wide receivers, Kenny Margerum, who was pushing for Gault's job starting in training camp.

For that matter, so does Gary Fencik come to play. He's a tough and smart free safety who's come a long way for not having much talent. Our defensive scheme the last few years under Buddy Ryan was such that Fencik was seldom put in a bad situation. He's getting up in years, and he can't run, so he's not much good in a one-on-one situation against another team's receiver. When the opposition does isolate him, like Miami did last year, Fencik can be had.

Fencik isn't afraid to get his uniform dirty. He isn't afraid to give you his opinions on anything, either. He went to Yale, and he lets you know it. I can live with Fencik, but we'll never be best friends. He's the resident genius. He even had the opinion that the Bears owed him something, like the chance to play in a Super Bowl, because he spent all those years playing with bad teams.

Well, I don't think the Bears owe Gary Fencik spit. He's played hard for them since 1976, but he forgets that the Dolphins drafted him first, and cut him, and it was the Bears who picked him up off the scrap heap. Gary Fencik, our resident genius, also was always one of the first guys to point at the offense as a reason why we lost. In his mind, the defense was always great, but the offense was inept. I reminded him of that a few times last year.

I respect him, though, and I'd better not get on his case too badly, because he's a Chicago-born guy who gets a huge cheer whenever he's introduced at Soldier Field. The fans love him, and he knows where the TV cameras are. He has a very nice smile.

Myself, I lean toward the more degenerate types like the offensive linemen. Kurt Becker and Keith Van Horne, the bookends, are two of my favorites. My first roommate with the Bears was Emery Moorehead, a tight end, a great guy. But the last three years, Becker and I have been together. We requested that arrangement, and management doesn't appreciate it, I don't think. They think he's a bad influence on me. Or maybe it's the other way around. Whatever, Kurt and I have a good time together, because he is a very, very sick man. He got hurt last year, and the Bears kept him on the inactive list longer than they had to, leading us both to feel they were screwing around with him. The Bears forget that Becker was one guy who turned our offensive line around. They used to be a timid bunch. Then he showed up from Michigan, getting down and dirty, preaching his theory of mutilation. One of Becker's favorite moments is when he can manhandle a guy, embarrass him, then spit on him. I *told* you he was sick.

Van Horne is in the same mold. If I were in a jam, I'd call either him or Becker in a second. Especially if I needed some muscle. Van Horne went through a lot last year. His dad passed away not long before the Super Bowl and I know it affected Keith, because they were close. But Keith continued to play hard; there's another underrated guy, another guy who deserved to go to the Pro Bowl. I wish both he and Becker had gone to Hawaii with me, in fact, though I don't know if Hawaii would have liked the idea.

One of my newest friends on the Bears is Kevin Butler, our rookie place kicker. Oddly enough, when he showed up at the training camp, I was rooting for our veteran, Bob Thomas. Thomas has been around for a few seasons, and Ditka had tried to get rid of him once. But after a short term with the Lions, Thomas was a Bear again, anxious to be on a winner at last, just like a lot of other long-suffering veterans.

Bob was a lot different from me. He was religious, and personable. But I liked to listen to him philosophize. I'd sit on the buses, or wherever, and just turn up the volume. He was interesting, and I was pulling for him to make the club, even though everybody realized the Bears didn't draft Butler in the fourth round from Georgia so they could cut him.

Every time Thomas made a field goal in practice, I would cheer for him. I don't know if the coaches liked that. I don't know if Butler appreciated it, but he was keeping his cool, and eventually we began bumping into each other at the bars in Platteville, Wisconsin, our summer home. Butler was a little worried about his situation, but he didn't show it in his kicking. He never seemed to miss. The kid had no nerves, and he had a little brass in him, too. He wasn't afraid to get a little animated after he nailed a field goal, and if the other team didn't like it, tough spit. You have to have an ego in this game, and besides, Butler wasn't just celebrating himself. He made a habit of congratulating the guys up front, the guys who blocked for him.

Not surprisingly, Butler made the team and Thomas didn't. Thomas was older, didn't get the distance on his kicks that Butler did. Plus, despite a good percentage of field goals made, Bob had missed a few big ones in his time with the Bears. You don't last ten years in the NFL if you're not any good, and not long after the Bears dropped him, Thomas was picked up by the San Diego Chargers.

The choice of Butler, though, was another piece that fit perfectly. He had the personality that was just right for "The Kremlin's Team." Before long, we knew he'd be a fine addition to our team not only on Sunday afternoons, but on Thursday nights.

That tradition began the year before with Jimbo Covert, our All-Pro who was just born to play left offensive tackle. Jimbo thought it would be a good idea to get the offensive linemen together once a week for a few beers, a few more beers, maybe even dinner if time permitted. They're brothers in the bond, these guys. They slug it out in the mud, and never get any attention. Like Jimbo once said, if you decide to be an offensive lineman, you first have to decide to put your ego in your pocket.

Well, when I heard about the offensive linemen doing the town, I invited myself along one Thursday night, and I haven't missed a Thursday night since. Butler, in time, joined the brigade. Even Fencik showed up once.

The idea is that one guy picks out a place each week, we go there, and the guy who picked it out pays. You can run up a pretty fair tab. A good bill is $600 or $700. Once, I got lucky. I selected my favorite spot, The Prime Minister, in Northbrook, the same suburb where I live. The owner there, Gus Cappas, is a prince, and a rabid Bears' fan. When he saw us animals walking in, he decided that he'd buy dinner if the place was still standing. It was, by some miracle, and I got off easily with a bill of $250 or so just for drinks. The food was on Gus.

We don't accomplish a whole lot at these Thursday night gatherings, even when they stretch into Friday morning. But we do laugh a lot, which is what it's all about. We talk a little about football and a lot about nothing, but the whole idea is being together. Offensive linemen don't get the recognition they deserve, but on our team, we make a point of appreciating them. Van Horne and Hilgy got an automobile commercial on TV; how often do you see that, even if it was just on Chicago TV? Wally did his bit, too. When he broke Jimmy Brown's career rushing record of 12,312 yards in 1984, he presented each offensive lineman—and Suhey, who also threw a few blocks on his behalf—a shotgun with a gold plaque of thanks. Hilgy said he was so thrilled that he planned to mount it and put it over his fireplace.

"But first, I'll have to wait until Walter reaches fifteen thousand yards," Hilgy said. "Then he can buy me a fireplace, too."

Otis Wilson. There's another guy. He made himself into a great ballplayer. Otis, Singletary, and Wilber Marshall were our three linebackers, and I would take those three over any in the league. Otis, particularly, came into his own in 1985. Buddy Ryan could be pretty biting with some of his comments, and that probably bugged Wilson when he first joined us. Otis would think, then react. Can't do that. Game's too fast. You have to think instinctively, while you're reacting. Otis got that all settled and became a hell of a player. Like most of the defensive team, Otis really came to understand Buddy, too. Ryan had great personnel, but he also knew how to use his people. When the Philadelphia Eagles hired Buddy as head coach after the Super Bowl, we knew we'd lost a hell of a man. Buddy was not only a genius, he helped keep us laughing. He was sort of the absentminded professor, always joking. Then our receivers' coach, Ted Plumb, another good football man, another good man, went with Buddy to Philadelphia as an assistant. You can't forget what they contributed to the Super Bowl season.

There were other people, too, who didn't play but made things more fun. When I got down, the first person I'd see every morning to cheer me up was Louise Johnson, the switchboard operator at Halas Hall. Great lady. And Ray Earley, our equipment man, kept us loose, too. He's been with the Bears forever. He knows where a few bodies are buried. Even the secretaries in the office seemed to join the upbeat, slightly zany feeling we had.

I can't forget, either, Richard McMurrin, the superintendent at Halas Hall. We'd always see him bouncing around, cleaning things up. And when he didn't clean, he would draw cartoons of the players, then pin them up all over. Quite the talent.

Richard must have been quite a fan, too. I remember going out to the bus that Sunday morning before our last regular-season game in Detroit. There was a blizzard going on, but here was this motorcycle parked by the side of the hotel, with a foot of snow on it.

"Who would be crazy enough to drive that in this weather?" I asked Van Horne. The motorcycle belonged to Richard. He'd driven it all the way from Chicago through the snow to Detroit. After he watched us beat the Lions, he hopped on that little sucker and drove six hours back to Chicago. The next morning, there he was at Halas Hall, sweeping around like nothing had happened.

He had to be nuts. That's why he must have felt so comfortable being around the 1985 Chicago Bears.

SIX

From Second Street to Bourbon Street

Sick. Mean. Intimidating. Aggressive. Compassionate. Smart. Sick. If you asked me for adjectives to describe the 1985 Bears, those are the ones I'd use. (They are all adjectives, aren't they?)

I'd use "sick" twice for good measure, unless you wanted me to use it three times. We had some strange dudes on our squad. We also had more laughs than I can envision any team ever having. Our business was our pleasure.

Compassionate? That might surprise some people, because we were portrayed as being just a bunch of animals. But we felt for each other, and we felt for other people. A lot of us "animals" did a lot of things nobody ever knew about for charities and children. We were even compassionate toward our coach. I mean, when we sped by Mike Ditka the night of our game in San Francisco, and we saw him getting handcuffed for drunk driving by the state police, we felt some genuine compassion for the man. That's why we honked our horns in tribute.

Smart? There's another surprise, huh? We had that image of being just a gang of reckless fools, beating up on other teams and saying anything that came to our minds. But if you don't think it takes some brains, and some long hours of work, to go 18–1 in the NFL and win a Super Bowl, you're mistaken.

When we gathered for training camp in July at Platteville, Wisconsin, there was a lot of uncertainty in the ranks, mostly because of contract hassles between some players and management. I'm not much of a historian on the Bears, but I'm told that since the dollar bill was invented, this franchise has been reluctant to pay a guy an honest wage for an honest day's effort.

Mike Singletary was having problems, and so was William Perry, our No. 1 draft choice out of Clemson. That's when The Refrigerator was really huge. He was a whole kitchen. Al Harris, a regular linebacker, was also a no-show, and so was Todd Bell, a hell of a safety, also a Pro-Bowler. Bell had become a free agent in the off-season, for what that's worth in the NFL. We were waiting every day for some solution on those two guys, and we're still waiting. Harris and Bell sat out the entire season.

Even though we were unsettled in training camp, I could feel that the guys who were there couldn't wait to start playing. That's unusual, because practice in that heat is boring, aggravating. Yet, you could sense this feeling building, a feeling that really had been building since the last half of the 1983 season. We had won five of our last six games that year to finish 8–8. We were starting to get the idea that we were pretty decent.

The 1984 season didn't change our minds. We went 10–6 and then beat the Redskins in Washington in our first playoff game, an upset in most experts' eyes. Then we went to San Francisco for the NFC Championship and got whipped badly, 23–0. It turned out that game would be something none of us forgot.

I didn't take the plane ride back to Chicago that night in January, but I heard that a lot of my teammates were furious. They didn't like the way they'd played, they didn't like the way the 49ers had acted, and they said it would never happen again if we got another chance.

I got a dose of 49ers Mania myself. I stayed in San Francisco after the game. Our season had ended, so I went with Nancy to see her family, which lives only about three miles from the 49ers' training facility. I read the newspapers for a week after they beat us, and I wanted to vomit. The whole idea they were putting across was that we didn't belong on the same field with them. "Next time, bring your offense." One of the 49ers said that to us after it was all over. Steve Fuller, who had played really well in Washington, started again as quarterback for us at San Francisco, and it wasn't one of his better days, admittedly. Still, we were down only 6–0 at halftime. It wasn't like we were humiliated, but the 49ers went on to win the Super Bowl over Miami, so I guess they could afford to talk. And they talked. And talked. And talked. That whole scene stayed with us during the off-season.

As for myself, I was coming back from a bad injury. In November of 1984, we beat the Los Angeles Raiders—another indication that we were a team on the rise. But in that game, I went down with a lacerated kidney. That sidelined me for the rest of the year, which was brutal. The good news was that doctors said I still had any kidneys left. After all the beer I'd inhaled since shortly after birth, I wasn't so sure.

Anyway, I went to training camp feeling good. Great, really, I was in great shape. But I was anxious to get hit, to see how my kidney felt. I knew it was still functioning, because, after sweating for hours in July, if you don't replenish your body liquids, you'll never survive. That part was going well. All systems were go.

Our first exhibition game was against the Cardinals in St. Louis. All I wanted to do was play a couple series of downs. I'm not into exhibition games. Plus, I was trying out this new protective gear, a corset, that was designed to guard my poor kidneys from further abuse. It felt very awkward. It's hard enough to play football in the heat of August, even without a girdle. But I got hit on the first down, and felt okay. I was ready for the games that mattered.

During our time in Platteville, we'd relieve the tedium by gathering along the town's strip at night for a few beverages. The place with a lot of the watering holes was called Second Street. Before long, some of the guys had decided that our mission for the year would be "From Second Street to Bourbon Street." In other words, from Platteville in July to New Orleans in January. They had it all mapped out.

Unfortunately, our 1985 regular season opener wasn't all that pretty. We played the Tampa Bay Buccaneers in Chicago, and it was hotter than hell. It didn't take me long to realize that the corset wasn't going to last. It was too warm, too cumbersome. I'd have to switch to something simpler, something that would make me look like just a keg of beer instead of a barrel.

As it happened, we needed all the points we could get. Our defense, which had been ranked No. 1 in the NFL since the first week of 1983, gave up 28 points in the first half. We were down 28–17 at intermission, and, not surprisingly, our wonderful Chicago fans were booing. They had good memories, if not good manners. It hadn't been since 1977—when the Bears beat Kansas City 28–27 after trailing 17–0—that the team had rallied to win after being behind so badly.

But, we came back to defeat Tampa Bay 38–28. It was 133 degrees on the artificial turf, everybody was waiting to see whether we'd survive without Harris and Bell in the lineup, and even though our defense gave up 307 yards in total offense, we won. I completed 23 passes, a career high for me in the pros, and we showed good balance. We threw 34 times, and rushed 34 times. If that game did anything, it pointed out that on a day when our defense wasn't playing so well, our offense could still have enough to get the job done. I pointed that out to Gary Fencik, our resident genius, who might have been surprised that the other half of the Bears could save the defense on occasion, too.

On the other hand, there was Otis Wilson, our outstanding linebacker, saying after the game, "I wasn't worried. . . . I knew our offense could do it." What's this? The start of a new era?

Our second game, also in Chicago, was against the New England Patriots. Our defense was back to its usual form: great. Buddy Ryan, the defensive coach, said it was as good a game as his guys played all year. The Patriots keyed on Payton, just like they would in the Super Bowl, and he gained only 39 yards—or 12 more than the entire New England team. But we won, convincingly, 20–7. Shades of things to come, though I don't think we were figuring on meeting New England in New Orleans in January.

I know I wasn't. I was hurting again. My back was killing me. Why, I don't know. I'd done something to it, and I went into traction the night after the New England game. I wasn't too happy about that, especially since we didn't have much time to get ready for our next game—Thursday night in Minnesota, on national TV. On the Thursday night version of *Monday Night Football* on ABC, with Frank Gifford, O.J. Simpson, and Joe Willie Namath.

But, apparently, no Jim McMahon. Oddly enough, Namath came to Chicago early in the week to tape a halftime show about how I was doing, about how I was healthy again! I offered to be interviewed in the hospital, while I was wrapped up like a mummy in traction, but somehow I didn't think that would fit the story line too well.

Namath came to Chicago anyway, and we did some taping, at the house, then over at practice. I was sitting in the stands with him, watching the guys go through drills, and I guess this got some people mad, particularly Ditka. He has this thing that if you don't practice the week before a game, you shouldn't play the game. That's a ridiculous philosophy at the pro level, I think. Maybe in high school, you punish a player that way. But I wasn't missing practice because I didn't care about the team, despite what Ditka might have thought.

"Steve Fuller's playing tomorrow night in Minnesota," Ditka told me before we flew up there.

"Okay, if that's the way you want it," I said. "But, I can play if you want me. I'll be ready if you have a problem."

I wasn't exactly delighted about that development. The Vikings were also 2–0 entering the game; they had started the season well with the return of Bud Grant, their longtime head coach who had come out of retirement. The Metrodome was wired that night. National TV. All that stuff. And here I was on the sidelines. ABC had decided not to run that piece about me being healthy again because I wasn't healthy again. But I was healthy enough to play. Would I? I didn't know.

"I see you, I see you," said Ditka, who watched me throw well during warm-ups.

"Just gettin' ready if you need me," I said.

It had been so long since I'd played on national TV, I wanted my friends to know I could still play. Besides, it was a Central Division game against a team we were tied with. Just gettin' ready if you need me, Mike. Do you hear me, Mike? Mike?

He heard me again at halftime. We were down 17–9 and I got in his ear again. Maybe if I nagged him enough, he'd change his mind.

"Don't wait till it's too late," I said.

"I don't want you to get hurt all over again," he said, brushing me off. He walked away.

Meanwhile, I could see our guys confused on the sidelines, demoralized, worried. It was nothing against Steve. We just weren't moving the ball. He'd gotten sacked a few times, and we'd had the ball seven drives in a row in the Vikings' territory, but we'd gotten only three field goals from Kevin Butler. Meanwhile, Tommy Kramer, the Vikings' quarterback, was having his usual good game against the Bears.

"You've got to make a change," I finally said to Ditka, midway through the third quarter. I just came over and just stood in front of him.

Ditka looked over at Fuller, then me, then Steve, then me again. He then went and told Steve that it was nothing personal, but we needed a spark. He was sending me in to replace him. That was with 7 minutes, 22 seconds left in the third quarter. I felt badly for Steve, but I was glad as hell to get in there. On my first play, I took the snap and stumbled. A fine start. I almost fell on my face. But, I'd taken a few muscle relaxers for pain before the game and, to put it mildly, I was a bit drowsy. I regained my balance. The play was a fullback screen to Matt Suhey. But as I went back, getting my footing, I could see the Vikings were blitzing. The safety had disappeared. Willie Gault was open downfield. I threw it to him, then got nailed. All of a sudden the crowd was very quiet. I looked between all the legs and saw that he'd caught it.

Touchdown! A 70-yard TD!! Thank you very much. I was pumped. Now, we're down 17–16.

Wilber Marshall, who was well on his way to becoming a sensational replacement for Harris, intercepted Kramer five plays later and we had the ball at the Minnesota 25. On our first play from scrimmage, a bootleg, I looked deep and there was nothing open. My next choice was our tight end. He was covered. Then I saw Dennis McKinnon coming across. I was now running toward the line of scrimmage, and I flipped it to an open area. McKinnon caught it for a 25-yard touchdown! Two plays, two TDs!!

"Screw them all!" I yelled as I came to the bench. Ditka heard me, and he knew I was talking about him and his no-practice-no-play rules. The guys? They were going crazy.

We got the ball back on a punt, and McKinnon, who was

having a great game, caught two more passes to bring us to their 43. Then came another sandlot maneuver. I started rolling right on a play-action pass. I didn't think anything was there, so I ran back to my left, and saw Dennis cutting across the field. I threw it and he ran under it. Touchdown! Three TDs on seven passes inside seven minutes!!

"I don't know how you write a script for what you saw out there," Ditka told reporters after we won 33–24. Later in the season, somebody asked Mike Singletary about destiny, and he said that game in Minnesota told him it was our year. McKinnon said it was a miracle. Buddy Ryan said I must have eyes in the back of my head. With all the muscle relaxers I'd taken, I might as well have. I was very loose, very tired, but very excited. My back survived, and so did my leg, where I had developed some sort of infection.

"What is it?" a reporter asked me.

"Looks like gangrene," I replied.

I floated back to Chicago, with a few beers on the flight, and then went back into the hospital for a couple days. We had a while until our next game, and I was feeling pretty good. That game put us on the map, made people realize the Bears were pretty exciting for a change. The last time we'd been on *Monday Night Football*, when it really was a Monday night game, we'd lost at San Diego in 1984. I was hurt then, too. Does this sound like a broken record?

Ten days later, after our big win in Minnesota, we played the Washington Redskins at home and crushed them 45–10. I almost blew that one early, by throwing a stupid interception, but Willie Gault returned a kickoff 99 yards for a touchdown, to get us back to within 10–7. Before it was over, I caught a touchdown pass from Wally. Quarterbacks aren't supposed to do that, but if it works, why not? If all the other receivers are covered, and as long as I didn't fall on my ass—which I was worried about doing—why not? We were 4–0, the Bears' best start since 1963, and besides, we had the added enjoyment of watching Joe Theismann punt the ball for 1 yard!! Theismann, the Redskins' quarterback, was pressed into duty because of injuries to Washington's regular punter, Jeff Hayes. Theismann, deep in his own territory, cold-shanked it. Beautiful.

We made it 5–0 in Tampa by rallying from a 12–0 deficit to win 27–19. I threw the ball like a woman that game, particularly the first half, but not because I was out all night before, like Ditka thought. Besides, we were all gearing up for our game next week at San Francisco, our chance to pay them back for all their yapping.

We'd been looking forward to the San Francisco game for a long time. "Just give us a lead and we'll take care of the rest," Steve McMichael told me before the game.

We went out and scored on our sixth play, with Tim Wrightman catching a pass from 24 yards out. I ran back to the bench and looked for McMichael.

"Is that fast enough for you?" I said, laughing.

We ripped the 49ers 26–10 right in Candlestick Park, and my only regret is that it couldn't have been worse. But we did manage to insult them a little, just as they had insulted us the previous January, in the NFC Championship. Late in that game, as if to rub our noses in the dirt, 49er coach Bill Walsh used a lineman, Guy McIntyre, for a couple of plays in the backfield.

Ditka didn't appreciate it, and that's where it all began with The Refrigerator. We didn't even have a play in our game plan for him, but I had a sneaking suspicion Ditka might be just crazy enough, just angry enough, to try something. Sure enough, with time running out, here comes William Perry waddling onto the field and into our huddle.

"Gimme da ball," said The Fridge, all hyper.

Most of our linemen thought it was a joke, until they realized they'd have to block for this 325-pound mountain. They were afraid he would run right up their backs and crush them to death, but at that point, we were having so much fun we didn't much care. Fridge carried twice and it was hilarious. He just ran into a pile of tacklers, got hit, and all you could see were these two huge legs digging away in the dirt, like two tires spinning out. The 49ers were furious. We were roaring. We were also 6–0.

"Refrigerator Mania" really caught on the next week at Chicago, where we had a Monday night game against the Green Bay Packers. Ditka, despite his wine funk on the flight back from San Francisco, had planted a seed. He wasn't going to let it die. First of all, it was a way of showing his sometime annoyance Buddy Ryan that Perry was a useful player. Ryan, after all, had called Perry a "fat kid" and a "wasted draft pick" at camp. That couldn't have pleased Ditka, who has a lot of input on the Bears' college choices.

More important, though, Ditka felt that this thing with using Perry on offense would help. The genius was at work, and I can't argue with him. So, for the Green Bay game, we installed some set plays for Perry. He lined up at fullback a couple times and blocked Green Bay's George Cumby from here to Rush Street so Wally could score two touchdowns from short yardage. Perry was awesome; the crowd was loving it.

But the icing on the cake—I'm sure The Fridge wouldn't mind me using that phrase—happened in the second quarter. We were tied 7–7 and were down at the Packer 1-yard line. The whole stadium could smell something coming when William came rambling in from the bench to inform the officials of his presence, all 300-plus pounds of him.

"Number 72 reportin'. . . . Number 72 reportin'," he yelled.

The huddle was a little tough to control, because we were laughing again. The offensive linemen, fearing for their lives, were hoping it would be a pass play so The Fridge wouldn't trample them to death. But it was a run, and he went in to score. Talk about backfield in motion. Talk about the Bears.

Everybody *was* now, in Chicago and across the country. We beat Green Bay 23–7 to go 7–0 and America had a new hero: William "Refrigerator" Perry. People swore off their diets and went back to eating French fries. Fat was in.

The media crush really set in then, but all those reporters around us even when we were blowing our noses didn't bother us. We whipped the Vikings again, 27–9, then went to Green Bay and won 16–10. That was a tough football game; a dirty game, in fact. The Packers were still fuming about how we'd shown them up in Chicago, as if the Green Bay–Chicago rivalry needed any more fuel. It's one of the fiercest in the NFL; plus, this was another game in our division, probably the last one we really had to win to stay comfortably in first place.

When we arrived at Lambeau Field, there was a sack of manure waiting in our locker room. That was some Packer fan's way of telling us what we were full of. On the second play, Ken Stills of Green Bay blasted me. A few minutes later, Mark Lee ran Wally out of bounds by our bench and was ejected for unnecessary roughness. I think Wally will be the first to tell you that one reason it looked so flagrant was because he grabbed Lee's jersey while they were falling down. Lee couldn't have let go, even if he'd wanted to.

The worst cheap shot came from Stills, also in the first half. He really creamed Suhey after a whistle. I like good, hard football as much as anyone, but that was brutal. The Packers showed no class. But we kept our cool pretty well, and won a real slugfest. We couldn't have done it without Wally, who was fabulous. He gained 192 yards. And The Fridge added to his legend by catching a touchdown pass. I was worried he'd drop it, but he surrounded the ball like it was the last double-cheeseburger on earth.

The play was a fake to Wally, and God help me if Perry had dropped the ball, because Emery Moorehead was wide open. The Packers were expecting something else, but as soon as Perry moved into the open, I heard one of their guys yell, "Oh, shit!" It was too late. William was in the end zone, doing his dance. He didn't stop shaking until he got back to the bench. I've never seen what 325 pounds of Jell-O looks like, but after watching Fridge celebrate, I have a mental picture.

Forrest Gregg, the Packer coach who had to have instigated all the cheap stuff his players were doing, went crazy when that happened. I patted Perry on the ass, which isn't too hard to find, and then I turned to the Green Bay sidelines to flip Gregg the bird. Then he went crazy all over again. We went to 9–0.

And I went right to the trainers' room. I had injured my shoulder in the San Francisco game, and it was getting worse all the time. In fact, if we hadn't been playing another division game after the 49ers game, I might have sat out that one. I was really in pain, and I never thought I'd ask not to play, but I did then.

My arm was really bothering me, so much so that the Bears even had me scheduled for surgery. The shoulder was inflamed, it was throbbing, and I was pretty miserable. Very restless. I didn't want to go under the knife, because that meant I'd have to skip the playoffs. So I waited it out, took some medication, saw a couple different doctors, and missed three games.

Fuller took over and beat Detroit 24–3, Dallas 44–0, and Atlanta 36–0. I especially enjoyed watching the demise of the Cowboys, and how Texas Stadium emptied early, like somebody had yelled, "Fire!" Late in that game, the few thousand Bears fans in the crowd just took the place over. Having little else to do but cheerlead and stay out of Ditka's way, I couldn't help but look over at the Dallas bench often. So many sad faces. What a shame.

With that destruction—somebody called it "Ditka Does Dallas"—we clinched our division, a formality since we had an 11–0 record. Mike was being mobbed for interviews before and after that game because of the obvious angle: Ditka, the pupil, against Tom Landry, his teacher.

Ditka did have some spare time to tell people he thought I wasn't involved enough in the team, or whatever. Maybe that explained why we weren't having much dialogue. If he thought I didn't care, he was wrong—again.

I wanted to play in our thirteenth game, another Monday night, at Miami. But Ditka stayed with Steve as his starter. There was another story line for that game—the Dolphins had been the last team to go through an entire season with a perfect record, 17–0 in 1972. Now, we were coming into the Orange Bowl to make a run at their mark. They didn't want it to happen. Besides, they were in a dogfight to win their division.

Looking back, maybe the fact that we lost to the Dolphins was a blessing. It proved that we weren't invincible, though I don't really think we were getting big heads or anything. We had the division locked up, and if we weren't really ready for the Dolphins, maybe that was why.

Dan Marino, their quarterback, had a big game, and he wasn't hurt by a couple breaks. I mean, when you bounce a pass off a guy's helmet and it goes for a touchdown, you know it's your night, right? I threw the ball freely in warm-ups, and wound up coming into the game when Fuller had to leave with an ankle injury early in the fourth quarter.

There were no miracles that evening. We lost 38–24 and Ditka had a nice little argument with Ryan. They were always at each other's throats. I don't know why Mike let that happen. If a guy builds the NFL's best defense, like Buddy did, why not leave him alone? Let the man do his thing, Mike, and worry about the offense.

I started the next game at home against Indianapolis, and we won 17–10. Of course, the writers who expected it to be 77–10 called me "rusty." Thanks, fellas. We were much better the next week in beating the Jets 19–6. Then we wound up at Detroit with a 37–17 win for a 15–1 record. Hurry up, playoffs. We were all getting antsy.

I look back at our season like this. We had a turnaround game in Minnesota and another in San Francisco. By turnaround, I mean one that we wanted to win more than most, maybe had to win. The game in Green Bay was the last of them, in a sense, although it would have been nice to win in Miami, too. Our game in New York against the Jets wasn't a must, but it was against a good team, with the playoffs upcoming. That helped calm down all the worrywarts who felt we had "peaked" too soon.

So, we were all looking forward to our first "big" game in two months, our first postseason game, against the New York Giants at Chicago. January in Soldier Field. We knew it would be miserable for us, but it had to be worse for the visiting team. I wasn't worried. But then, I don't worry easily.

It was cold, all right, that first Sunday in January. Windy, too, and that might have been one cause for the most amazing punt this side of Theismann's feeble effort. Sean Landeta, the New York punter, prepared to kick from deep in his end . . . and he whiffed!! Have you ever tried to hit a golf ball on the tee and missed all but two dimples? That was Landeta. Shaun Gayle, who will be a star for the Bears someday, scooped it up and recorded a 5-yard return for a touchdown.

We led only 7–0 at the half, but that was enough. Butler missed a couple chances to give us a bigger lead, but he was off, for the first time all season. I wore gloves and had good luck throwing spirals into the wind, New York's Joe Morris was held to 32 yards, and we won 21–0. I think the people were starting to get the idea that we weren't the 1969 Cubs then, or even the 1984 Cubs. We weren't going to let down.

It was a lot warmer, but still windy, the next Sunday when

we hosted the Los Angeles Rams for the NFC Championship. I was even less concerned about them than the Giants for some reason. Maybe I believed what everybody was writing, that the Giants were mirror images of the Bears—rough, tough, oblivious to the weather—and the Rams were not.

Whatever, we won 24–0. Defense was great. Eric Dickerson, the Rams' rushing leader, didn't do much better than Morris, gaining 46 yards. I wore gloves again and threw spirals again. Why, I have no idea. I don't throw many spirals without them. I might wear gloves forever, I announced. I might wear gloves to bed. I didn't sleep much that night, however. The guys had a few beers after the game at our usual outpost—in the underground parking lot at Soldier Field—while the traffic cleared. Then Nancy and I took a suite at a downtown hotel because I had to appear on one of those early-morning network shows. My rear end was aching, and I was very tired, but I could handle it. One more game to go. No reason for a big celebration yet.

But it looked like the guys knew what they were talking about back in Platteville during July. We'd made it from Second Street to Bourbon Street.

SEVEN

Fame and Fortune

Let me tell you a story about Monopoly money.

I was sitting at home one afternoon last March, just relaxing. Nancy and I had plans to meet some friends for dinner and a few beverages at that favorite spot of ours, The Prime Minister, a couple miles from where we live. The phone rang. It was Steve Zucker, my representative of the last few years and a good friend.

"Jim, do you have any pressing plans tonight?" he said.

"Nothing heavy," I told him, "Nance and I are just going to the Prime for dinner."

"Well," Zucker said, "I just got a phone call from a guy who's in a fix. Refrigerator was supposed to make an appearance for this company at a cocktail party tonight, and he's had to cancel at the last minute. His wife, Sherry, is expecting. Anyway, they want you to take his place and they'll pay you ten thousand dollars for what amounts to about an hour. What about it?"

"Nah," I said. "I'd really just like to lay low tonight."

Steve said fine, he'd tell them no. Less than two minutes later, the telephone was ringing again.

"Jim," Zucker said, "they won't back off. They're up to fifteen thousand."

"Nah," I said. "I really just feel like having dinner and a couple beers tonight. Can't they find someone else? A lot of the other Bears are in town."

Steve hung up. Two minutes later, *b-r-r-r-ing*.

"Jim," Zucker said, "they'll pay you twenty thousand. All you have to do is show up by six-thirty. They'll send a limo to pick you up. They said they'll have you back at The Prime Minister by eight o'clock. It's crazy."

It was crazy, all right. I looked at Nancy.

"I don't really feel like doing this," I said. "I want to just go to dinner, but for twenty thousand dollars, I guess I can miss the hors d'oeuvres, huh?"

And off I went. Bizarre but true. I went to this function, and was back at the restaurant in time for a nice quiet meal, with twenty thousand dollars in my pocket. A few years ago in college, if I had twenty dollars in my pocket to go to dinner, I thought it was a big deal. Now, they're shoving twenty grand in my face, and I don't even want to do half the things people are asking me to do.

That's what I mean when I say it's like Monopoly money now. I don't keep track of my finances, because Steve is so good at it and I trust him completely. But he said that in the first couple months after the Super Bowl, I made close to a million dollars for doing commercials and making appearances and that sort of thing.

Steve also said that I could have made a million more, but he didn't even bring half the offers to my attention. He just knows how I am, so he rejected them right off, or put them "on hold." You know, don't call us, we'll call you. One of the strangest proposals came from St. Louis.

"We've got a letter here from a secretary," Zucker told me. "Actually five secretaries. They want to know would you come down there and have lunch with them for one hour. They'll pay you fifteen thousand dollars."

"Female secretaries, I presume?" I said.

"Yeah," he said. "And then she goes on to ask, if the other four girls decide not to pay that much, would you consider having lunch with just her? Sounds like she has more than lunch on her mind."

"You mean dessert, too," I said.

And so it went after the Super Bowl. I had a chance to play a drug dealer in *Miami Vice,* but we turned that down for two reasons. First of all, it would have taken too much time. Secondly, I wanted Keith Van Horne and Kurt Becker, my two wacko bookends from the offensive line, to have parts, too. The TV people said no, so I said no.

We had another movie proposal that would have been worth more than $400,000, according to Steve, but that would cut about five weeks out of the off-season. No way. I live for those months, so I can play golf. Can you imagine me standing around putting makeup on when I could be there in the fresh air teeing it up?

There were too many other deals to even describe. Steve said he was getting forty or fifty a week. He placed a limit of one hour per appearance—autographs, shaking hands, making small talk, whatever—and set the price at a minimum of $20,000. Not because he knew I wanted that kind of money, but because he wanted to scare off as many as possible. I'm not on the fame kick. I'm not on the fortune kick, either, even though I used to think that $500 for an appearance as a rookie was all the money in the world.

As it is, I'm doing okay. Steve started handling my affairs after Jerry Argovitz, who was my agent when I got out of Brigham Young, and went on to become an owner with the Houston Gamblers of the United States Football League, so he couldn't also do work for clients such as myself. Plus, I liked the idea of someone local, and Steve is not only terrific at what he does, he knows everybody in Chicago. There isn't once when I go someplace with him that a dozen people don't come up and start talking to him about this or that.

Steve is a very rich man, but he's not impressed by himself or what he's worth. He charges me a very reasonable fee for what he negotiates, but I've never felt that he's working for me. With me, yes. For me, no. I consider him one of my best friends outside football, and that's the way it should be. We talk too often on the phone, spend too much time together for us not to be friends, too. I don't think he looks at me as only a client; at least, I hope not.

Zucker also has his hard-nosed side, though. Near the end of my first contract with the Bears, a three-year deal that was nothing to write home about, they came to us wanting to "extend" my contract. The Bears don't "renegotiate" because it's against club policy, but they do "extend." I think we're talking semantics here, but it was a small miracle that they even bothered to do anything. Jerry Vainisi, who succeeded Jim Finks as general manager, said that the team realized I was their "quarterback of the future" and the first "real" quarterback since Sid Luckman in the 1940's. Vainisi, and Mike Ditka, too, said that I was the kind of quarterback they wanted to keep around for a while, to build a team on.

So Steve went in and laid a big one on them. The difference between the Bears' idea of showing appreciation for me and Steve's idea was night and day, but, after weeks of not talking to them, we came out with a very good contract, at least at the time. The way guys are getting paid by some other teams now, it might be time for Steve to go in there again. There are a few quarterbacks who never played for a Super Bowl champion who are making a lot more money than I am.

Starting in June of 1984, I began a five-year contract starting at $600,000, and then graduating by $50,000 each season. In addition, I got a $350,000 signing bonus.

In any case, I'm in pretty good shape. I want to take care of Nancy, and put away enough money so our kids—Ashley, who's three, and Sean, two—will be able to go to college and not have any financial worries the rest of their lives. That's all that really matters to me. Steve says I spend hardly anything, and he's right, I suppose.

I can't stand to shop, and practically every bit of clothing I own, Nancy buys for me. I tell her if she sees something that she really likes, buy it for me, because I'll never buy it for myself. I own one suit, and hardly ever wear that, except maybe to weddings and funerals. If it was up to me, I'd wear jeans 365 days a year, unless I could get away with wearing nothing. It's a little too nippy for that in Chicago.

We don't take any wild trips or collect cars or live extravagantly. We're planning to build a nice home near where we live now, in Northbrook, but other than that, the only things I buy regularly are dinner, beer, and golf balls. I don't think I'm what you would call a fancy guy, although Nance can have whatever she wants. The kids aren't hurting for diversions, either. Ashley has more gadgets than Toys-R-Us. In fact, I've told her that her room looks like Toys-R-Ashley. My children can have whatever they want, on one condition. I don't ever want them shoving it in the face of a friend that they might have more toys, or more clothes, or whatever. I'll spoil my kids, but not to that extent.

All of this probably surprises some of my many critics in the media, who think I'm the biggest brat of all. That's fine. They're not going to change their opinion of me, and I'm not going to change my opinion of them. Or at least, most of them. Believe it or not, there are some sportswriters and sportscasters whom I respect. It's just like any business. There are jerks, and there are good people. You see that on a football team. You see that in the media.

If it was up to me, I'd be able to go to a hockey game, or walk into a movie, and never be noticed. But, that's not very easy anymore. Nance and I and some friends went to a show last spring. I just wanted to sit there and relax, but I could hear people around me saying, "There's Jim McMahon. . . . Jim McMahon's here!" I wished I could have just been invisible, but I had no chance. I imagine a lot of other so-called celebrities feed off that star stuff. If Joe Theismann went into a movie theater and wasn't noticed, he'd probably be crushed. I could see him grabbing the public-address system.

"Uh, ladies and gentlemen, while you're enjoying Out of Africa *here tonight, you might want to know that Joe Theismann, the quarterback for the Washington Redskins, is seated in Row 6, Seat 12."*

I'd rather just blend into the scenery. I could never understand why fans would stand around for hours on line just waiting to get somebody's autograph. I went to one opening of a shopping center last March in Kokomo, Indiana, and I signed so many autographs that I needed to bandage my fingers after it was all over. Unbelievable. I didn't particularly enjoy it, but I had about 20,000 reasons for doing it.

My friends in the media will read that and it will just confirm their notion that I'm greedy and self-centered and out for as much as I can get. They don't know that I gave my best friend, Pluto, $40,000 for the down payment on his house, and I don't care if I never see it again. They don't know that I paid off the mortgage for a buddy in trouble back in Utah, and flew him and his family to the Super Bowl. They don't know, and I don't really care if they never know. I'll give you an example of what I go through with some of these people in the media. After the Super Bowl, Steve got a call from a lady from the Sunshine Foundation concerning a young football player in Elgin, Illinois. He'd suffered the same kind of kidney injury I had with the Bears, only the doctors told him he couldn't play ever again. He was down and depressed and this lady wondered if there was some way I could get in touch with him, call him, send him a football, something.

"Let's go," I said to Steve.

So I drove out there one afternoon. I didn't realize until I got there that they had called one of the Chicago TV stations about my visit. There was a camera crew there. I wasn't too excited about that, but it wasn't my business what the lady did. I was there to talk to the kid, not the TV cameras, and I told them that. They could take all the pictures they wanted, but no interviews. I only wanted to talk to the kid.

Well, they got their noses out of joint. I never saw what they put on the air, if they put anything on the air at all, but I'll bet it was something to make me look like a jerk. "Jim McMahon ignores press again." Something like that. I don't care, really. All I care about is that I made that young guy feel better about life. He was surprised I showed up, we had a nice chat, and that's all that matters. Maybe a million people watching TV that night thought I was a jerk, but I know one guy who didn't. I can handle that.

My "fee" for that appearance was a twelve-pack of Moosehead beer. The lady had asked if she could do anything for me, and I told her what was closest to my heart. That I didn't charge her for taking the time would probably shock some of the media mongers, like Jeannie Morris of WBBM-TV in Chicago. She's the former wife of Johnny Morris, once a damn good player with the Bears and the chief sportscaster at the same channel.

They both come across as though athletes in town owe them an interview whenever they show up. Particularly Johnny. Well, I don't feel I owe them. And I had one go-round with Jeannie last season that resulted in her getting the last word, the last jab. That's one thing about the media. They always have the final say.

She came running after me one day at Halas Hall, wanting me to do a tape of some sort. I said I didn't have time, which I didn't, because I had to go to practice. She got angry. Then she followed me up to the field and started chasing me down, even when I was doing some laps. If I were her, I would have filmed me running laps for posterity, because that was a collector's item. But, no, she had to have her interview. Now, I got angry.

After practice, she chased me all the way to a car, where I was getting ready to leave. I was in a hurry. She started yapping at me, and I flipped her the bird. Not too smart, but that's the way I felt. Well, that night she went on the air and showed me giving her the finger. She said something like, Jim McMahon thinks he's No. 1, and if you don't think so, just ask him. Then she ripped me for not giving interviews unless I'm paid for them. That's another lie they like to spread about me.

Well, I can produce a whole stack of newspaper clippings proving that I talk an awful lot to reporters, and I haven't gotten a check from a newspaper yet. I imagine that myth started because every Thursday morning during the season, I do a short little phone-in at eight-fifteen on WGN Radio with Wally Phillips, who has the highest-rated talk show in Chicago. Steve said it would be good exposure for me, so I did it. Plus, the station's sports director, Chuck Swirsky, is a good guy who's been good to me. I did it partly as a favor to him.

I also did it because when they phone, it serves as a wake-up call for practice. The fact that I can do the broadcast stark naked, lying in bed, is a fringe benefit. I always wanted to do a show in the nude. When they start having those telephones with TV monitors on them, I'm in trouble. Anyway, I did get paid for that, which probably is what got Jeannie and her buddies mad. What they never told their audiences was that my salary was a measly $100. Yeah, I sure am greedy.

But, that's life in the fishbowl. It boggles my mind, the effect that the media has on the public. The power is awesome. I cut my hair funny in training camp, and all of a sudden, I was a punk rocker. MTV wanted me to do a show.

That's another offer we turned down. I cut my hair, and all of a sudden, I'm a rock star. Well, I listen to a rock station often in the car, but I don't collect tapes or records and I wouldn't know a lyric from a song if I fell over it. But the media decided I wanted to be a punk rocker, and the public believed it, so I was a punk rocker. If I wear glasses and a mustache to training camp next year, what's the media going to say then? That I want to be Groucho Marx?

I wouldn't mind all that clout the media has if it was used correctly. I don't mind when reporters write what they see instead of what they think they see. It's not that I'm afraid of criticism. When I play a lousy game, who's the first one to say so? Me. Even the press people who hate me have to admit that. It's just that so many of them try to get nosy and impose their own opinions on what they write. I had a Moosehead while visiting that kid at his house. For all I know, on the news that night, they made me out to be not only a jerk, but an alcoholic, which is another of their misconceptions about me.

I guess that's what burns me most. This business of them coming in with a preconceived idea of something and never being willing to change it. Like that time when that fool sportscaster in New Orleans said I called the women all "sluts." The rumor got knocked down in a hurry, but even as I was up there explaining how it was false, I knew that a lot of those press people wanted it to be true. They wanted to nail me. Again. And they will, over something, I'm sure.

Part of the cause of that, I imagine, is that reporters like to be catered to. But I don't kiss anybody's rear end, and I'm not going to start with them. A few of the members of the press I know and respect tell me that I'm "good copy," that I make a good story. So what happens? The same writers who rip athletes for being too dull and too careful with what they say then rip me because I don't care what I say; because, on occasion, I can be funny or ridiculous. What is it they want? Do they want me to fill their notebooks with my thoughts about acupuncture? Or would they rather have me never talk about anything? One way, I'm too arrogant, too brash. The other way, I'm too smug, too withdrawn. You can't win. Not that I'm trying to win with them. I'll continue to play with their minds as long as I'm around, and they can let me have it as long as they're around. That suits me fine. One columnist, Bernie Lincicome of the *Chicago Tribune,* uses me as his favorite punching bag. There was that game in Green Bay last November. I was hurt so badly that I had to go into the trainers' room for treatment right after. I missed the next three games. But because I didn't come out for interviews, he thought that I was pouting. Pouting? We won the game. My problem was I couldn't lift my arm. That didn't change his story, though. He had it preconceived that I was pouting, and he'd have written that if I'd been carried out of there in a coffin. But I didn't want him to know I was hurting. And, in the end, I don't want most reporters to know me, period. They can write all the fiction they want.

I once looked down on reporters because I figured, how can they write about a game they never played? How can they really understand it? I still feel a little bit that way, but not as much. I've mellowed. I realize a good movie critic doesn't have to have been an actor, a good political writer didn't have to be president. Believe it or not, I can also feel comfortable with a writer who obviously is a different breed of cat from me. Like Mike Janofsky of the *New York Times.* He's always got a necktie on, and his newspaper isn't on my required-reading list. Very, what's the word . . . erudite? No comics. But Janofsky knows what he's talking about, he's fair, he's thorough, and he doesn't take my words and print them in his words. He quotes me correctly. He's not alone. There are a lot of good, conscientious people in the press. Just be fair. If I throw an interception, write that I threw an interception, that it was a terrible pass, a stupid play. Don't write that I threw an interception because I was out all night, when I wasn't, but you feel like writing it anyway, so you write it.

I guess, generally speaking, the media is a pretty conservative, buttoned-down lot. They aren't quite ready for someone like me, wearing outrageous clothes and saying outrageous things just for the sake of a few laughs. Most reporters, I've found, are lacking in the humor department. They come to the stadium on Sundays like they're covering World War III instead of just a game. You'd think it was them who were going to get tackled, not us. I mean, if I can have fun with football, and it's my bread and butter, why can't they have fun with something that isn't their living? They get paid the same whether we win or lose, but you wouldn't know by some of their attitudes. So serious, so self-important.

We have one guy in Chicago who doesn't cover the Bears regularly. He does NFL football, the whole league, but we see him often enough. Well, the way he walks around, you'd think that sixty thousand people are buying tickets to come out and see him. The game can't start without him, or so he would have you believe.

But these are the people who are responsible for creating the images of athletes for their readers and viewers and listeners, whether the images are true or not. Then you go to a golf tournament in the summer and you get placed with a complete stranger in a pro-am. You have a good time for eighteen holes, you have a drink, and then he hits you with the big one.

"You know, Jim, you're a pretty good guy," he'll say.

"Thanks," I'll say. "What was I supposed to be?"

"Well," he'll say, kind of uneasily. "After some of the things I've read about you, I figured you'd be a real jerk. But, you're not."

So it goes. I've tried my best to cooperate with the media. I've had my moods, like anybody else. The picture they've painted of me isn't always flattering, but if they keep writing that I'm not a person worth knowing, and then fifteen thousand people stand in the rain to get my autograph, well, maybe fans don't believe everything they read after all.

I don't pretend to understand what makes the media the way it is, or what makes fans fans. I don't think I could ever live my life vicariously through a team, or an athlete, but if rooting for the Bears helps some people release their tensions and get through another day, swell. That's what the entertainment business is for, and that's why we are entertainers.

As long as I'm in professional football, as long as I'm a so-called public figure, I'll have to deal to some extent with people I don't like and people who don't like me. I've thought of becoming another Steve Carlton, the pitcher for the Philadelphia Phillies who doesn't talk to any media, ever. It's intriguing, but hiding might take more energy than doing what I do now. My office is the football field, and that's where the fans can boo and the press can rip. But my private life, my family, and my friends are out of bounds and always will be. Only a very few people will ever get to know Jim McMahon the person instead of just Jim McMahon, quarterback, Chicago Bears. I can guarantee that.

You can have the group scenes, too. If I can pat a kid on the head because he can't get out of his wheelchair, and that makes him feel better about himself, then that's worth more than getting good ink, or having some TV guy stroke me by saying I played a great game, or sitting in some department store hearing people squeal over you because they think you're a rock star when you're not, or something superhuman when you're only human.

People think I'm strange, maybe. I think people are strange definitely. Imagine someone wanting to pay $15,000 to have lunch with me? Do you get the salad bar with that?

EIGHT

Hello, Bears

As nearly as I can recollect, I was back in Utah lying on a couch and sipping a Bloody Mary when I first became a Bear. It was Draft Day, April 1982, when the NFL selects the best student-athletes from the college ranks to turn professional. I was ready, willing, and able, having done my time at Brigham Young, which is not to say that I graduated.

I really wasn't thinking about the Bears. They had a 6–10 record the year before, and were picking fifth. The Baltimore Colts had done even worse, and were looking for a quarterback, so I had some indication I'd be going there. Maybe that's why I got into Bloody Marys early; I wasn't too excited about Baltimore, although I just wanted to wind up *somewhere* and get it over with. The draft was televised, and there were a few camera crews standing by my couch to record my reactions if and when my name was called. When Baltimore tabbed Art Schlichter, a quarterback from Ohio State, I did not cry. I didn't think he was worth a damn, and in years to follow, he proved me right. He played in the Big Ten and got all that publicity, but the Big Ten is nothing special. Every year they send a team to the Rose Bowl, and every year they get beat. Great, I thought. Schlichter can go to Baltimore and freeze his butt off.

Little did I know that Chicago was even colder. I didn't have much of a handle on the Bears' tradition. I had spent most of my life out west, so we never saw them much on TV. I had some images of the Bears . . . the Monsters of the Midway . . . Dick Butkus . . . Gale Sayers. I had also seen the movie, *Brian's Song*, about Brian Piccolo, the Bears' running back who had died because of cancer. But that was about it.

I really didn't know anybody in Chicago, either, except Kenny Margerum, a real good guy whom the Bears had drafted the year before out of Stanford. I met Margerum, a wide receiver and a damn good one, at the Hula Bowl in Hawaii a few years before and we had become friends. He was always telling me, "Wouldn't it be great if we played together on the Bears someday?" I never really gave it much thought.

Then, the Bears telephoned me at the house before it was their turn to choose. They were after a quarterback, too. They asked me how I felt. I said I felt fine. And I did. Wouldn't you, lying on a couch sipping on a Bloody Mary and watching TV? I wasn't exactly uptight.

"Chicago Bears select Jim McMahon from Brigham Young University," came the announcement over the tube.

Lights! Action! I was interviewed and all that, and then told to fly to Chicago for a press conference. The Bears paid for my plane ticket, but my agent at the time, Jerry Argovitz, had to buy his own. Argovitz had the reputation of being a tough negotiator, so this was the Bears' way of taking an early stand, I suppose.

"I think he can compete," Jim Finks, then the Bears' general manager, told the press. The Bears had two veteran quarterbacks, Bob Avellini and Vince Evans, but Finks was saying that the best guy would win the job. I thought that was fair, which is more than I could say about their contract offer.

When I arrived at O'Hare Airport to make my debut before the Chicago media that I would come to know and adore, the first representative from the Bears I met had chicken grease all over his shirt. His name is Mitch Friedman, and he's still the official team photographer. I thought to myself, This is the big leagues? They draft me No. 1, they fly me in from Utah, and they send this little fat guy with chicken grease on his shirt to greet me?

Oh, well. That's life. I figured Mitch was probably a decent enough fellow. He probably just liked to eat chicken. Or spill chicken. Whatever. I was tired and a little groggy myself, because my thirst for Bloody Marys had continued on the flight to Chicago.

The media was gathered at Halas Hall in Lake Forest to hear my first words of wisdom. I told them I thought Vince Evans lacked consistency and that I wasn't going to lie down, that I'd fight for the starting job when training camp began. I also said that the Bears had placed a lot of faith in me and that I wanted to give them everything back. Pretty cool, eh?

Mike Ditka, who was entering his first year as head coach, said it was a pleasant surprise that I was still available "because he was by far our highest-rated quarterback." Since then, Ditka has admitted that when he saw this guy with sunglasses, carrying a beer can, and chewing tobacco show up at Halas Hall, he knew he had someone different on his hands.

"Real different," said Ditka.

But, he also said that, when it came time for the Bears to make their pick, "we didn't even need five seconds. McMahon was our man. We're thrilled to have him."

Jim Parmer, the Bears' director of collegiate scouting, said a lot of wonderful things about me, too. Even George Halas, Papa Bear, sounded happy that his team had drafted a quarterback in the first round for the first time since 1951. "I'm well pleased," said Halas. "He possesses something Evans doesn't possess. That's the touch."

There was another minor item I didn't possess, either. That was a contract. And in time, it became apparent that the Bears thought I'd accept all their praises instead of money. Cash, not compliments, buys groceries. Argovitz had been around the block with the Bears, so he knew. He'd handled Margerum's contract, and blasted Finks for being behind the times. I could sense that we were in for some real unfriendly conversations.

The first meeting was a disaster. The Bears' opening offer was something like $60,000 for my first year, $70,000 my second, then $90,000 and $100,000. Outrageous. Four years, peanuts. We wanted more like $100,000/$150,000/$200,000, plus a million-dollar signing bonus. Obviously, we were quite far apart. Things were going so badly that they decided to bring me into the meetings. Finks was there, plus Argovitz, plus George Halas. They didn't invite Mitch Friedman, probably because he was out somewhere buying some chicken to spread on his shirt.

I guess I was supposed to be awed at my first session and my first glimpse of George Halas, but I wasn't. I had heard that he'd given a lot of money to charity. Maybe, I thought, that's why he didn't have any money left for me. Maybe, instead of telling him I was his No. 1 draft pick, I should have posed as somebody from the Red Cross. Maybe that would have killed some of the moths off his wallet.

As it was, Halas was just someone else I had to meet. I wasn't really aware of the fact that he was one of the founders of pro football, or that he had started the Bears' franchise on a shoestring. All I could figure out was that he still had the shoestring.

"Young man, we're offering you more money than we've ever offered a rookie," Halas said.

I didn't know what to make of that. Here was this legend sitting in a chair, with his slippers on, getting all hot and bothered at me.

"If it was up to me, you should go up to Canada to play pro football," Halas went on. "If we give you two hundred bucks a game, you're overpaid. You've got a bad arm, a bad eye, bad knees, and you're too small."

All of a sudden, the Bears weren't so thrilled that I was still available in the draft.

Argovitz and I had another problem staring us in the face. The collective bargaining agreement of the NFL Players Association was due to expire on midnight July 15 of that year. If I didn't sign with the Bears by then, I was looking at the possibility of having to sit out the entire year. That was the summer before the players went on strike for seven weeks during the regular season, so things were getting more than a little tense. If rookies didn't sign before that deadline, they were cooked. They couldn't even go to training camp, which began July 24. Veterans could negotiate after the July 15 date, but not us rookies.

I had another possibility if the Bears wouldn't budge. The United States Football League. George Allen, who had been a big success with the Washington Redskins, had taken over the Chicago Blitz of the new league. I flew out to see him in Los Angeles and was floored by his offer. A great contract, much better numbers than the Bears, plus a percentage of the ownership. I guess Allen figured it would be a big coup for the Blitz and USFL if they could snatch the Bears' No. 1 pick away.

At that point, I didn't care so much where I played. I just wanted to play. Everything we did with Allen was verbal. I told him that if he would put it in writing, he had a deal, because neither Argovitz nor I saw much sense in beating our heads against the wall with the Bears I could sign with the new league, and still go to the NFL at some future date if I wanted to.

Well, as it turned out, Allen never got back to us with anything in writing. He never got back to us period, and it wasn't because we didn't try to get back to him. I don't know what he was thinking. Maybe he figured that he'd throw out all those fancy figures at us, then we'd wait until past that July 15 deadline, and he'd have us by the short hairs because it would be too late to sign with the Bears.

Whatever, it wasn't looking too optimistic. I remember talking a couple of years later to Steve Young, who had followed me as quarterback at Brigham Young. He received this unbelievable offer from the Los Angeles Express of the USFL. Like, $40 million. He asked me what he should do. I told him it was no decision. Grab it. He said he was concerned about missing out on all the prestige of playing in the NFL. I told him, hell with the prestige. Whatever he missed out on he could buy with that kind of dough.

This advice was coming from yours truly, a guy who never had that kind of deal with the USFL, and from a guy whose potential boss was telling me that I'd be overpaid if I got $200 a game.

I tried to steer clear of the crossfire between the Bears and Argovitz during the spring and summer of 1982. There wasn't much progress to report, and Jerry got angry. He trotted out some of the salaries other draft choices were getting, guys like Schlichter, guys who were drafted well below me and were making a lot more.

"It's insulting," Argovitz said. "The Bears showed how little they think of Jim by offering him fifteen thousand dollars if he can make the rookie first team in the NFL. I think that's really great. Finks said the Chicago offer is the second largest they ever made to a Bear player, second only to Walter Payton. Either Finks is a liar, or there are a lot of underpaid players on the Bears. I bring this all up with Jim McMahon and what does he say? He says it looks like he'll be playing a lot of golf this summer."

And what did Jim Finks say?

"No comment," Finks replied. "I don't have to say anything. Mr. Argovitz is doing all the talking."

And so it went on.

But we were getting down to zero hour, I wanted to play, and it was obvious that the USFL alternative wasn't going to pan out. So, I signed with the Bears for three years at $100,000 for the first, $150,000 for the second, and $190,000, plus an option year. The Bears opened up their shirts and their hearts fell out.

Argovitz had eleven clients that year, including nine in the first round. None signed until the last minute, and I got the least money of all even though I was the highest pick. I don't blame Jerry for the low figures. He did the best he could, considering the Bears' stubborn attitude and their repeated claims that they weren't making any money, that they were a poor family operation that couldn't afford what some of the other teams in the league were paying. We even had a third party involved—Carl Severe, a friend of mine from Provo, Utah, whose house I had stayed at for a while when I was in school. He said that Finks and Argovitz needed a marriage counselor because things were getting pretty ugly. I guess. I remember one time Jerry got so hot at Halas for pulling the poverty routine that he hit the Old Man with a novel proposal.

"Okay, Mr. Halas, if you can't afford to keep up with the salaries in the NFL, if you can't pay Jim McMahon what he's worth, I have an idea," Argovitz said. "I'll be back with a check for fifty million dollars tomorrow morning to buy the Bears." Halas, I guess, nearly lost his dentures.

"Uh, oh, um, we can't do that," Halas stammered at Argovitz. "No matter how difficult it is to run this team, we want to keep it in the family. The Chicago Bears are not for sale."

No kidding, the Bears weren't for sale. By this time, I had talked to a few people, and it turned out that Finks wasn't lying. They really did have a lot of underpaid players on their team. They still do. So does every other team in the NFL, but don't get me started on that just yet.

So, there I was, officially a Chicago Bear, and an officially angry Chicago Bear.

Argovitz wasn't too happy, either. That rule stating I had to sign by midnight July 15 was a bunch of baloney. It was the first time it ever existed, and the last time, too. It wasn't even a rule, because Marcus Allen fudged with it and went and signed with the Los Angeles Raiders. So did Darrin Nelson, who signed with the Minnesota Vikings. I was caught in the middle with a cheap Bears' management, a players' association contract that was expiring, a war between two leagues that was driving players' salaries up—well, at least most players—and my desire to just get the thing over with, to play football.

Argovitz had one parting shot at them. Just before I went into the Bears' executive offices to sign the contract, he showed me a note. It stated that I had signed the contract under severe "duress, distress and coercion." It stated also that, even after I signed, I reserved the right to sue the Bears, to revoke the whole deal, and start from scratch. Become a free man. An ex-Bear before I ever played a game for the cheapskates.

"Will you sign this?" Argovitz asked.

"But of course," I said.

When I went in and did my contract, Argovitz then wheeled around and presented copies of the warning letter to Finks and Halas.

"What the f—— is this?" said Finks, who crumpled the thing up and threw it away.

I don't recall any reaction from Halas. He might have been on the floor again, looking for his dentures.

When we opened the door to the outside world, the first guy to come rushing in was Margerum. He was so happy that I'd finally signed and ended the ordeal that he started screaming at the top of his lungs. Then we exchanged high-fives. Halas had to be taking in this scene and wondering, What the hell have I gotten myself into? Who are these nuts?

I wasn't at all happy about the outcome, and I said as much to the reporters, who were also waiting outside. It was over with, I signed, I was going to play. But I was pissed. That's what I said, and they printed it and they showed me on TV, and that was the start of my love affair with the Bears' front office.

That night, Margerum and I went out and got completely overserved along with Dan Neal. He was a veteran center on the Bears whom I didn't know at the time. But it didn't take long for us to become good buddies. He liked his beverages, too. With my first training camp not too far off, I was, I regret to report, not exactly in the best shape. I would not have been mistaken for a Greek god. I had gotten married that May, gone off to Hawaii, come back and played a lot of golf. The way our contract talks weren't progressing with the Bears, I figured I wouldn't even be in training camp, so I didn't pump too much iron. I had a little extra padding around the middle.

Wouldn't you know it? One of the first tasks I had to perform was the mile-and-a-half run, in sweltering heat. It was grotesque. It was embarrassing. It was, as I look back on it, pretty hilarious.

I managed to finish in twelve minutes and thirty-seven seconds, not an especially swift clocking for someone who's supposed to be an athlete. I beat one other player, Noah Jackson, whom we called The Buddha for obvious reasons. Noah, who was built along the lines of The Refrigerator, came in twenty seconds behind me, just under thirteen minutes. If my memory serves me correctly, the winner was Pat McCaskey, who was then the team's public relations director. That shows you what kind of condition the Bears were in.

But I was in no position to talk. I got sick during the third lap, then I started getting delirious, then I started seeing things, like cold cans of beer in front of me. I was drenched from perspiration, and not too sure about ever making it in without an ambulance.

As it was, I walked the last 30 yards, which probably didn't please the authorities too much. When it was over, all I wanted to do was lie down, because my legs felt like spaghetti. Freddie Caito, the trainer, rushed over to me with some wet towels. He must have thought I was about to collapse. Then Ted Plumb, one of our assistant coaches, ran over to me.

"Son," he said, "you've got some work to do." No shit, Sherlock.

It must have been quite a sight for the reporters witnessing my effort. I don't know if there are any film clips of my dashing 12:37 mile and a half, but if there are, they won't have to bother with any slow motion. The whole thing was in slow motion. They could have captured me with a Brownie and the snapshot wouldn't even have been blurred. Vince Evans and Bob Avellini must have loved it. Here was this hotshot out of college who was going to fight them for the quarterback job, and I was near death. I wanted to just find a bed, some ice for my legs, and something to drink.

"You were awful out there," Margerum said that night at a Lake Forest bar, The Lantern, where I had found something to drink.

"I took one look at you wobbling around that track," said Kurt Becker, "and I thought to myself, 'Who the ——— is this spastic?' "

Despite my brutal display, the Bears gave me a uniform,

No. 9. I learned in a hurry that it had belonged to John Roveto, a place kicker who was pals with Steve McMichael, our carniverous defensive tackle. He came up one day and just pushed me, to test me.

"Get away from here," I said, acting tougher than I was feeling. "You might get hurt."

"Oh, yeah?" McMichael said. "How do you figure that, kid?"

Then he took his helmet, smashed it into his forehead five or six times, and just walked away. *Oh,* I thought, so *these* are my new teammates.

Avellini started the first two games of the 1982 season, at Detroit and New Orleans. Evans came in for Avellini against the Saints, and then I started the second half instead of Evans. That wasn't very fair to Vinny, but he was on his way out with the Bears. His star was fading; he eventually wound up in the USFL.

After the Saints game came the strike, and we didn't resume playing again until November at home against Detroit. I started that game, we won 20–17, I was awarded a game ball, and I started the last six games, too. We wound up 3–6. I was the United Press International NFC rookie of the year, and my 80.1 passing rating was the best in NFL history for a rookie, especially a rookie who ran one and a half miles in twelve minutes, thirty-seven seconds.

I was benched briefly, about a third of the way into the 1983 season, but still started thirteen out of fourteen games. We rallied to wind up 8–8. We were coming on, and Ditka started to cool down a bit. Whenever I threw an interception, or an incompletion, I didn't feel like he was breathing down my neck. You can't play football with a guy looking over your shoulder. You can't do anything that way. I missed seven games in 1984, because of a variety of injuries, not because Ditka had reverted to his rotating quarterback system. I was his man, for better or worse, as long as I could stay healthy and as long as I didn't have to enter any more track meets.

Which reminds me. After that rookie season, we haven't ever had to run one and a half miles in training camp. I guess after they saw what I did to that event, they decided to retire it.

Wise move. It's been a lot more fun to play for the Bears since then, although some things never change. Every time I see Mitch Friedman, he's still wearing his chicken dinner.

NINE

The System

Late April of 1986, I was making an appearance near Chicago. I ran into a reporter there.

"Who would you like to see the Bears pick in the NFL draft next week?" he asked.

"I'd like to see us draft an owner," I said.

After he lifted his jaw off the ground, he started writing feverishly in his notebook. There I was again. Good copy. Opening my big mouth. Once in a while, I wake up in the morning and regret something I've said or done. But that doesn't happen often, and that day in April wasn't one of those times. I said exactly what I felt.

On the one hand, I think I was put on this earth to be a Bear, that it was meant to be. You know, predestined that I would wind up with a crazy bunch of guys like we had in 1985. Lots of talent, lots of laughs. I include Mike Ditka in there, too. Can you imagine me getting mad at Tom Landry in Dallas on the sidelines and telling him "——— you"? Or Don Shula in Miami? No way. I wouldn't last in either place.

Then on the other hand, I wonder how long I'm going to last playing for the Bears. I think I might rather retire early than play the rest of my career for the current president of the Bears, Michael McCaskey. He and I don't see eye to eye on a lot of things, the most important of those things being professional football.

Michael McCaskey doesn't have any qualifications to operate the Bears, except his name. He went from Yale to Harvard to running his own consulting firm to running the Bears. He took over as president and chief executive officer in November of 1983, and before he got his feet wet, he was jumping around our locker room, in January of 1986, with a Super Bowl trophy. He must think he's the reason we won. That's scary, but I'm afraid it's true.

His dad is Edward McCaskey, the chairman of the board, who probably doesn't have all that much power anymore. Ed married George Halas's daughter, Virginia, so that's the family connection. I don't have much to do with Ed. He's a good old guy who comes down to our locker room every once in a while and drops some cigars off in my stall.

I try to have as little as possible to do with his son, Michael, who became the big honcho not long after Halas's death. The party line is that the Bears needed a bright and fairly young guy to take charge, so Michael got the nod. I don't deny that he might be bright, or that he is fairly young. What I wonder about is his feel for or knowledge of football.

Unfortunately, Michael is regarded as something of a hero among fellow owners. He took a stand against Todd Bell and Al Harris at the beginning of the 1985 season. He wouldn't pay them what they wanted. They didn't play one minute for us. And still, we won the Super Bowl. What does that make Michael McCaskey with his peers? A genius. What nobody ever remembers is that we were very lucky with injuries in 1985. The holdouts of Bell and Harris left us dangerously thin, but we got by because of superior attitude and talent, if not depth.

The precedent McCaskey established can mean only trouble. If he believes that the Bears—or any other team, for that matter—can afford to let good players not play, for the sake of "fiscal responsibility," then that creates problems. You can deplete a roster only so much. You can continue to think that "we'll win with what we have" only so long. Pretty soon, you're back to being an ordinary team.

It would be a crime if the Bears were allowed to become that. We not only had the best team in football in 1985, we had the youngest. That means, if management works to keep the team together, we could become a dynasty, like the Pittsburgh Steelers, who won four Super Bowls in the 1970s. We could do that in the 1980s, if McCaskey wants to pay the price.

Somehow, I don't think he's up to that. My gut reaction is that he'll take our championship and rest on his laurels—or rather, our laurels. When he came onto the field in the fourth quarter at New Orleans, smiling from ear to ear, I got that eerie feeling that he felt it was his team, his leadership, that did it all. That's why I went out of my way to avoid him, and I wasn't alone. Walter Payton was right beside me, and he was just laughing at McCaskey.

Most of us just laugh to keep from strangling him. The Bears who won Super Bowl XX were not a happy bunch of players. Michael McCaskey might think we won because of him; he'd be offended to learn that most of us felt we won in spite of him. I don't know exactly where our payroll ranked in the NFL. I've heard anywhere from eleventh to twenty-fourth. You can always play with figures like that, because of deferred money and signing bonuses and things like that. But, I know we were low, considering what we accomplished.

You can't maintain a championship team by operating that way, but I think McCaskey is planning on it. He could have signed Richard Dent, our Super Bowl MVP, our great defensive end, to a contract last year. But the Bears kept screwing around, and he wound up playing for $90,000—a brutally low salary for any regular in the NFL, let alone an athlete of Dent's caliber. They thought they had him backed into a corner; he turned that around by playing so well. But Dent wasn't the first player to go through that with the Bears, and I'm afraid he won't be the last. Bell sat out the 1985 season after making a measly $77,000 in 1984, when he went to the Pro Bowl. The Bears made him an offer with a significant increase, of course, but obviously, it wasn't significant enough. For a guy who loves to play football like Todd Bell to sit out an entire season tells me he'd had just about enough of their pinching pennies. This wasn't a rookie making $77,000, remember. This was a guy making $77,000 during his fourth year in the league!

I saw this type of thing happening from my first day with the Bears. I saw a guy like Calvin Thomas working his fanny off and making nothing—$20,000 in 1982, he said. I saw offensive linemen slugging it out day after day and earning maybe $100,000. It doesn't take a mathematician to figure out that you don't need many of those to bring your payroll down.

I'm not complaining about my salary, remember. I know there are quarterbacks like Marc Wilson of the Los Angeles Raiders making more for accomplishing less. But I'm complaining about some of the other things I see around the Bears, things that can't continue—unless, of course, management is happy with one title team every twenty-three years.

Our practice facilities, for one, aren't what they should be. We have one grass field behind our headquarters at Halas Hall in Lake Forest. That's swell until winter sets in, and around Chicago, during football season, we tend to get a lot of winter. So, when there's a foot of snow outside, we have to pile into a bus and go scrounging around for some high school gym in the area, just to get loose. We need an indoor facility. Mike Ditka said all last year that we needed one of those more than anything, more than any one player. But, unless it's "fiscally responsible," don't hold your breath for McCaskey to build one. My teammate Kenny Margerum has a brother who's big in real estate. We had the idea of buying our own tract of land around Lake Forest, constructing a football field with one of those all-weather bubbles over it, then leasing it to the Bears. Knowing the Bears, though, they'd let us go ahead with it, then back off because they couldn't afford to rent it.

As it was, during the first of two weeks before the Super Bowl, we had to go to Champaign, Illinois, to use the University of Illinois' bubble. And when it wasn't there, we were either driving around the state looking for a gym or heading off to Suwanee, Georgia, to use the Atlanta Falcons' plant. The word among the players was, if you want to be a Bear, you'd better get enrolled in one of those frequent-flyer programs. With all the money McCaskey saves, he could at least afford to buy his own bus company. Only if it was "fiscally responsible," of course.

If it's not that kind of nickel-dime stuff annoying us, it's something else. During Super Bowl week, we were all allowed to buy twenty tickets each, at $75 a pop. That's nice, except we were told we couldn't get more. And many of us needed more. The New England Patriots players told us they had the option to buy thirty each, but we could only get twenty. I don't know where all the tickets went, but I'd guess the McCaskey family had its hands on them, for all the cronies and buddies coming to New Orleans.

There were certainly enough of them in town. Management arranged a charter flight to go to New Orleans on the Friday before the game. That was the one for our wives and children. Problem is we were permitted to use only one seat each. So if you wanted to bring your wife down plus your kid, your kid had to be able to sit on your wife's lap, or vice versa. That didn't work for Becky Cabral, the wife of Brian, one of our linebackers. She had to send their seven-year-old son on a separate flight, even though there were open seats on the charter. And most of the occupied seats were taken by the McCaskey clan, which might explain where all the game tickets went. All I know is that Walter Payton, the greatest player in football history, busted his tail for eleven years in Chicago so he could go on a New Orleans street corner and get scalped for the extra tickets he needed. Management didn't have any available.

After the season, management invited the players to go on a boat cruise with some fans, who paid for the privilege. I have no idea who made what off that shindig, and I don't want to know. I suspect that Michael McCaskey didn't do it out of the kindness of his heart. I realized that when I heard that people like Ray Earley, our equipment manager who has worked long hours for many years, was also "invited" to come along. If he had $2,000 lying around. Here's a guy who has to wash our jockstraps for a living, but they can't pay for him out of loyalty. If you don't think that bothers the players, even players like myself who are making a pretty good buck, you don't understand what makes a team tick. I told management I wanted no part of their cruise, and they were furious. Jay Hilgenberg, our center, told them he was too busy to go. He got a letter accusing him of becoming "greedy." Jay was preparing to get married last summer, but I suppose that didn't matter. If the cruise had been a reward to players and staff, that would have been one thing. But, it was a fan outing, probably for profit and fun. Imagine Michael McCaskey calling anybody greedy!

It wasn't much different from our postgame party in New Orleans. It would have been nice to have a little season-ending bash for players and families. Instead, McCaskey rented this huge ballroom. I went down there for two minutes and noticed it was an intimate gathering of about three thousand people, most of whom I'd never seen before. I took a peek and left, then went up to the players' wing of the hotel, where most of us were sticking together, like we had all season.

I'm not exactly sure of Jerry Vainisi's place in all this. He's probably a pretty good general manager, even if he does do some silly things, like tell us we can't watch soap operas on the locker room TV during our spare time. I suspect Jim Finks, who preceded him, might have been a decent GM, too. But they probably have had their hands tied.

I think I know where Ditka stands, though. More than once during meetings he's hinted that the Bears' ownership is this franchise's danger zone. It was Halas, remember, who hired Ditka.

I'll say this about Michael McCaskey and all his fellow owners. The way the NFL is, there's no reason to spend money because there's no incentive to win. Whether you win the Super Bowl or win one game all year, it's all pretty much the same because of revenue sharing. The twenty-eight teams in the NFL all get the same huge sum from the TV networks at the start of the year, so why pay to have better players if it doesn't matter? Unless you're really committed to excellence, why spend money? Just finish 8–8 every year and turn a profit. Walter Payton could tell you better than anybody about the system. He became a free agent a few years ago, meaning he was supposedly available to sign with any team. But no other team bothered to offer him a contract; no other team even called. After all, he's only the all-time NFL rushing leader. Who could use him?

Well, I don't think you have to know any more about the owners and how they operate. They're all in this together to make a bundle, and the more Michael McCaskey cries about how running the Bears as a family operation is just "marginally profitable," the more I'd like to get someone qualified to look at the books—the real books. It's a business, a big business, and if it's such a bad business, why didn't George Halas accept an offer of $50 million to get out?

I can't say I really blame the owners, though. Complete free agency is legally ours. The baseball players have proven that. They move around to the highest bidder, but I don't see that sport crumbling like the football owners say theirs would. All I see is baseball breaking attendance records every year, and TV ratings getting bigger and better.

But, in contrast to baseball, our association, our version of free agency, is a complete joke. We've been sold out before, and we'll probably get sold out again. If a player like Walter Payton becomes a free agent and leaves the Bears, the franchise that signs him has to compensate the Bears with draft choices, high draft choices. In other words, it's free agency in name only. It's restrictive. It's a farce. But the owners have to love it. Wouldn't you? We went on strike for seven games during the 1982 season and got absolutely nothing for it. Nothing. The owners hung tough, and all we did was lose paychecks. They have us in the palms of their hands. First it was Ed Garvey. Now Gene Upshaw is our union chief. He seems to me to be a puppet. The owners tell him to jump, he asks them how high and when. It's brutal.

I'd like to see us do what the baseball players did. They were getting bad wages and few rights, so they went to a steel mill in Pittsburgh and hired Marvin Miller. He might not have known a lot about baseball. He didn't have to. What he knows is how to negotiate with management on behalf of labor. And what a job he did.

As it is, here we are in professional football, the most popular spectator sport in America. The best, too, I think. And yet, we've got players playing for much lower average salaries than players in baseball or basketball. Meanwhile, the average life span of a career in the NFL is something like 4.3 years. That's all the time we have to make it. *We* are the game, not the owners. But the owners will be there for years; we're here for 4.3 years.

We've got another session due with them in 1987. That's when this current contract expires. We'd better be ready to wage war then, and not with squirt guns, like we've been using until now. We have to do something. We have to get something. We have to stay tough and stay together. We can't crumble like we always have in the past.

The owners have brought up drug testing as a big item, not necessarily as part of our next negotiations. They say that the drug problem in the NFL is a real issue, but I'm not so sure they aren't bringing this up as camouflage. They think that if they keep saying that drugs are the main thing that has to be solved, they can make us forget about free agency. I don't think it's going to work, not for a minute. There are too many players getting angry about being underpaid, and with the United States Football League on its deathbed, we're about to lose our only alternative. The USFL decided to move from a spring–summer schedule to the fall–winter of 1986, right in competition with the NFL. Much as I hate to say it, the USFL doesn't have a chance.

I don't mean to brush off the drug situation. We had one player last year with a real problem, James Maness. He knew he needed help; we told him he needed help. We caught him doing cocaine in the locker room. He'd come into meetings with a roll of toilet paper, his nose was running so bad. Eventually, he went into a rehabilitation clinic. Worse yet, Maness came to our mini-camp in May of 1986 and tested positive again for drugs. He was gone. It was a terrible thing to see. But I get around a little bit, and talk to a lot of players, and I just don't think the drug problem is that widespread. Steve Grogan, the quarterback for the Patriots, said that big exposé right after the Super Bowl about drugs on the New England team was wildly overblown. I believe him.

I still think it's awful, what drug abuse can do to a human being. I also think—and this may sound awfully cold—that if a guy in any walk of life wants to kill himself, he's going to do it. The owners, while they're testing us for drugs, might want to test fellow owners. Not only for drugs, but for booze. There are some owners in this league who are so drunk on Sundays, they can't make it up the stairs of the stadium. These are the same people who worry about what goes into our bodies. I guarantee, some of the stuff they inject us with on Sunday mornings so we can play is worse than smoking a joint. But painkillers and needles and pills don't count, I guess, because it's the clubs that administer them.

Drugs might affect a small portion of the players; free agency, or lack of it, affects us all. If the owners want to give us the free agency that's overdue, that's legally ours, in exchange for drug testing, I'd be all for it. I'd be for giving them almost anything in exchange for free agency, because if we don't have it when my contract is finished, I might just be the one to challenge the whole rotten system. I might be the one to topple the cards.

If I could put up with all the B.S. in the meetings we have now, if I thought it would do some good, I'd get involved in players' association affairs. But the cold fact is, the longer it goes on, the more chance we have of getting screwed around. I have very little faith in the union, and its leaders. I'd like to see my representative, Steve Zucker, get in there and take charge of the thing. He'd have those owners running for cover. He'd get to the bottom of what it means to be "fiscally responsible" in a hurry.

By the time my contract is up, I'll probably have enough money to last me. But I'd like to fight for the guys who don't speak up, who can't afford to speak up. Guys like our Mike Hartenstine, who plays hard for eleven years, never says a word to rock the boat, and makes maybe $200,000 a year. That's who I'd go to bat for, and if it meant me being blackballed, well, those sixteen Sundays a year without football would hurt, but I'd get by. We need somebody to stand up. We just can't continue to be wimps. How can a group of players be so strong on the field, like we are in the NFL, yet so weak off the field?

I'd like to play pro football forever, or at least until I'm forty, because I enjoy it so much. But, I can't see doing it for the Bears unless Michael McCaskey sells the team. He takes a lot of the fun out of the game. Can you imagine a bunch of players sitting around the night they win the Super Bowl and talking about how much they'd like to be traded? If everything the Bears do is so fair, why do we lose so many players, so many coaches? If they give us as much money as they can, like they say they do, why did they come after me to "extend" my contract a couple of years ago? Because they knew they'd taken me to the cleaners and because they knew I knew. Maybe I scare them because I speak my mind. If that's the case, good. They need to be scared.

But that doesn't make it fun for me. Winning is fun. Being around the guys is fun. Dealing with the nickel-dime stuff management puts you through is no fun at all. There are other teams as bad as the Bears. And then there are teams like the Raiders. Al Davis, their owner, lets his players be themselves, as long as they play like hell on Sundays. John Madden, who used to coach there before he became the great broadcaster he is now, was the same way.

You see it every year. Players who can't fit the mold or the image of other teams go to Los Angeles, and Davis turns them into winners. Davis doesn't want robots. He wants football players. He's a different cat, which is why he's on the outs with the NFL and Commissioner Pete Rozelle. He challenged the system and won. He challenges them every day. I said earlier I sometimes think I was born to be a Bear. That doesn't mean I wasn't born to finish a Raider. I hope you didn't take me wrong when I said earlier that the Super Bowl was a bore. It was great to win, great for the guys, great to prove ourselves to our doubters. But that doesn't mean we didn't have to put up with a lot of petty stuff. We're entertainers. We were entertaining the whole country the way we played. And here was our management getting together with the league to outlaw headbands. Silly, but true.

The system is full of politics, and while winning a Super Bowl can cure a lot of things, it can't cure everything, like a tissue-thin players' union or an owner who thinks small instead of big. A lot of people figured the Bears would show up at the White House to meet President Reagan after we won the Super Bowl, but I knew it would never happen—unless Michael McCaskey could have convinced all the players to take a bus to Washington to save money.

Either that, or President Reagan would have had to send *Air Force One* to Chicago to get us. Free of charge, naturally.

Walter Payton and me sharing a quiet moment on the sideline. As you can see, Wally likes headbands, too.

Wally is the ultimate prankster, even at a formal team photo session —*especially* then. Here he's giving me goat horns from his seat in the second row.

When the 1985 Bears got their heads together, they *really* got their heads together. My roomie Kurt Becker and I are doing some of the head butting we enjoyed so much.

Thursday night follies. From left to right, Mark Bortz, Keith Van Horne, Kurt Becker, and Andy Frederick. Obviously, the bystander in the background thinks we're outrageous. Obviously, he's correct.

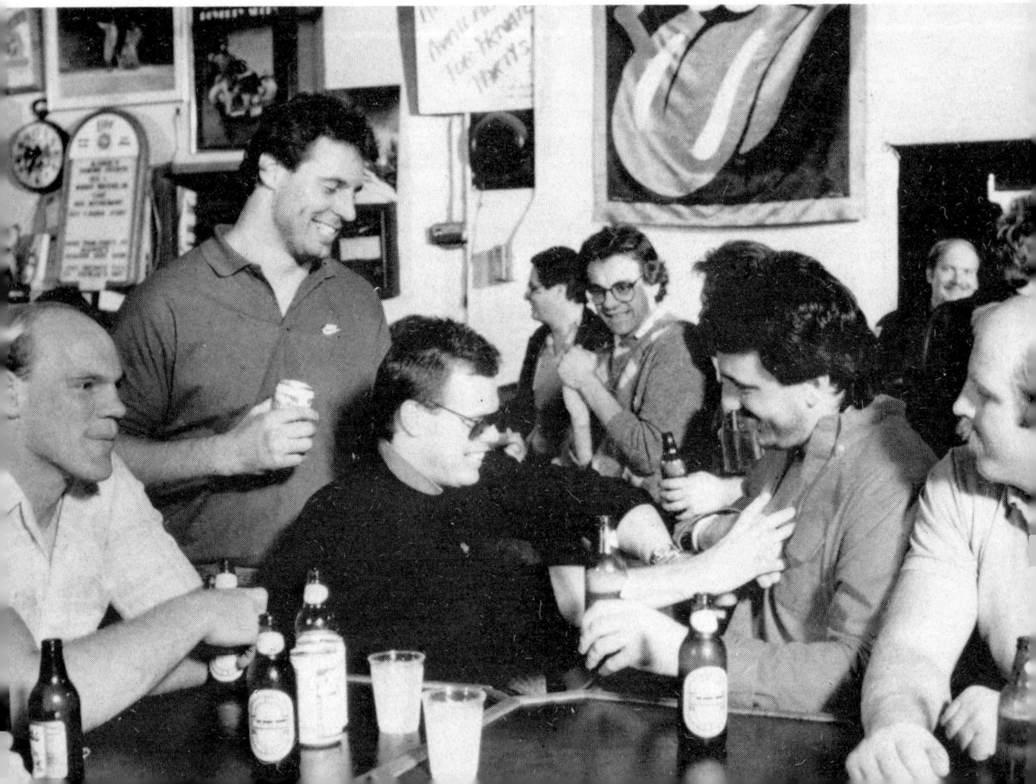

Coach Mike Ditka looking at me early in the 1985 season, trying to figure out where all my hair went. This photo is proof we can see eye to eye.

That's me with the football. This is just another reason why golf is my favorite sport.

Relaxing on the bench in Dallas after Coach Ditka told me he didn't like my outfit. We creamed them 44-0 with Steve Fuller at quarterback.

This shot at a Super Bowl press conference is a rarity. I'm at ease with a few hundred of my close friends in the media and I'm wearing a necktie.

William Perry, the Refrigerator, is holding on tight here—he thinks I'm a cheeseburger!

Running toward the Patriots' end zone in Super Bowl XX. We ended up there a lot that Sunday.

Michael McCaskey, Bears team president, being interviewed by NBC's Bob Costas after Super Bowl XX while Commissioner Pete Rozelle looked on. McCaskey is holding on to his newest friend, the Super Bowl trophy. They have been inseparable ever since.

Here we are at Disney World. Ashley and Sean seem to be having fun, but Nancy looks like she just lost her traveler's checks.

Our Christmas card 1985.

The famous golfer in the photo is:
A) **Jack Nicklaus** B) **Sam Snead** C) **Arnold Palmer** D) **Jim McMahon**
I hope you guessed "D." This really *is* my favorite way to swing.

I told you sometimes football is war.

T E N

Crazy Me, Crazy Position

I'd like to play quarterback in the NFL for twenty more years. To accomplish that, however, I'll have to live twenty more years. That could pose a slight problem. As I've said often, when my number is up, this body is going right to the Smithsonian Institution. They'll have a nice time examining all my scar tissue. I'm not going to list all the injuries I've had since I started playing this crazy position, because I don't want this book to turn into an encyclopedia. But I will say that lacerated kidney I suffered in November of 1984 was a dandy, and not only because I couldn't drink beer for three weeks. It also scared the hell out of me, and I don't scare easily.

We wanted badly to beat the Raiders that day, and we did. But you know what they say about the Raiders. Win or lose, they make you pay because they're so rough. They made me pay. I've been hit harder, actually, but the way I got spun around and nailed in the side by a helmet right there where I was vulnerable . . . well, I knew I was in big trouble.

I was rasping, croaking when I got back to the huddle. I

called an audible designed for Willie Gault, but when I threw the ball, he wasn't there. It got picked off. Willie had a good reason for not being where I thought he'd be. "I couldn't hear you, Mac," he said. "Are you hurting?"

Was I ever. I told Steve Fuller to be ready. Eventually, I couldn't take it any longer. I went in and tried to urinate. Like grape juice. I was bleeding internally. I jumped right in the shower, and must have stayed there for an hour, because I knew where I was going, I wouldn't shower for a week. I was headed to the hospital for a prolonged visit.

"What's the score?" I asked the ambulance driver on the way.

"You're up 17–6 in the fourth quarter," he said.

That was the only thing that made me feel good. In the emergency room, I was in unbelievable pain, but they couldn't give me a shot until they diagnosed what it was. They thought it might be a cracked rib or a punctured lung. I kept babbling, "Kidney! . . . Kidney!" I wanted to sleep, but couldn't, because I hurt too much. They shot dye into me, and I vomited. They moved me, and I screamed. I must have been a real joy to be around.

After several hours, my mouth was so dry that I asked the nurse about a beverage. Specifically, a beer. She said no. Fred Caito, our trainer, still marvels to this day about the fact that I went three weeks without a beer, my longest stretch since shortly after birth. He didn't think I could do it. As it was, I got hurt on a Sunday, and didn't eat again until Friday. I splurged and had some Jell-O. That really hit the spot. By that time, I didn't have to worry about bodily functions. They injected me so full of morphine, my plumbing was shut down for a spell. A hand-delivered copy of *Hustler* magazine even failed to get me excited.

I spent ten days in the hospital, the rest of the winter sitting around going crazy, and then most of the spring getting ready for training camp—all the while hearing comments from people that I should retire, that my career would be over with another hit on my kidney, that my life would be over with two more hits on my kidney, and so on. At least if I'd have quit then and there, I'd never have had to deal with Buddy Diliberto.

But, as long as I'm playing quarterback the way I play quarterback, I suppose I'll be walking the thin line between danger and self-preservation. You can't play thinking safety first. That's when you first catch your lunch. Besides, if it's your time to get hurt, it's your time. Heck, Tommy Kramer of the Vikings blew his knee out while he was standing on the sidelines.

My first major injury came when I was a sophomore in high school. A couple of gorillas fell on me and my arm locked. I snapped it back in place, locating the dislocation, but I crushed all the tendons, so I couldn't lift the sucker for weeks. I came back sooner than I should have, and started throwing sidearm. Since then, it's been one thing or another.

I always used to tear up my ankles for some reason. Had casts on them both at various times. I've broken my left wrist, my right hand, but not my nose. Nobody can get at it, it's so small. I've had three operations on my left knee and one on my right. I've split my chin wide open. I had cracked vertebrae, and a cracked tailbone. That was fun. I had to drive the car around while sitting on one of those plastic donuts, like a pregnant woman. There aren't many parts of me that haven't been wrapped in plaster at one time or another.

That's my style, though. And it's not because I like punishment. It's not because I'm a masochist. On most Monday mornings, I don't like the way I feel, sore all over, as though I'd spent the night in a cement mixer.

I can think of only one game during the 1985 season that I didn't take much abuse—the second game against Minnesota. I woke up Monday feeling as though I hadn't even played. And, after the Vikings read this, I'm sure that'll change the next time we play them.

Why do I get hurt so often? I think part of it is my style —as someone said, I fail to abandon my recklessness. The other part is that after I get hurt, I usually continue to play hurt. That just compounds the problem. It weakens everything else.

There's no safe place out there on the football field, though, and I'd rather be in the game getting bounced around than on the sidelines, twiddling my thumbs and arguing with Ditka about why my jeans are faded. It's not that I like contact; it's that I don't really mind it.

I love my linemen, and that's one reason why I roll up my sleeves like they do. As a toast to them. Also, our jerseys are so huge that you can swim in them. It's easy for somebody on the opposing team to grab hold. Our management must have a deal with the manufacturer—the more cloth they buy, the cheaper it is. But the myth about me being a closet lineman, me wanting to come back in my next life as a sweathog—it's not true. If I had a choice to be something other than a quarterback, it would be a receiver. Not only for the joy of scoring touchdowns. I don't mind the traffic. I'd be just like Dennis McKinnon or Kenny Margerum, sticking their noses into crowds, making blocks.

But, I'm the Bears' quarterback of the future—or so they tell me—and that's fine. It's the most important position on a football team. Everything revolves around you, which is the way I like it. I want to be in charge. I'd rather have it in my hands, whether we win or lose, because I feel I'm a winner. Everywhere I've played, we've won. That's a good feeling, being in command.

When I first stepped into the Bears' huddle as a rookie in 1982, I started screaming out orders, and letting guys know when I didn't think they were doing their jobs. Dan Neal, our center, took me aside and told me, "Jimmy, that's great

. . . we haven't had a take-charge quarterback like you here in too long. The guys aren't used to that, but they'll *get* used to it."

It was nothing I hadn't done before, in college or in high school. I'm not a holler guy in that sense. A quarterback isn't out there to be a cheerleader. You're not paid to stand there and say, "Let's go, team." The huddle is your office. You're there to run the offense. You have to have complete respect. Of course, you don't get that, no matter how much you act like Sergeant Bilko, unless you deliver.

Hopefully, my teammates on the Bears know that I'll do anything for them. Even if they don't like me as a person, they have to know that I'm not sitting back on cruise control with a nice five-year contract, going through the motions. I'll do anything for those forty-four other guys, and I hope those other forty-four guys feel the same way about me.

While a quarterback isn't in the huddle to say "please," it's a good idea to be a good listener, too. A two-way conversation doesn't hurt sometimes. I'll occasionally ask, say, a wide receiver if he was open on a previous pattern. Or, before I get down to calling signals, where you have to have everybody's undivided attention, a receiver might mention that he thinks he can beat the guy covering him. Inside, outside, whatever. If you take a teammate's suggestion, he damn well better be open. But, the flip side of that is, if a guy gives you an idea and you use it, he's going to work his butt off to make it click.

Above all, you have to inspire confidence in the team. If other players see you giving up, that's trouble. You can't come into a huddle like some wimp and say, "Well, maybe we should try this, fellas." That's contagious, just like it's contagious when they see a quarterback—supposedly the guy in the most skilled position—sacrificing his body for an extra yard or two. No matter what the odds, you can't come across as feeling hopeless.

There was only one situation I can remember last year that would even border on that. We were in the closing moments of our only loss at Miami. I had replaced Fuller, who was injured, and Walter Payton was shooting for his eighth straight game of one hundred yards or more. That would have broken the record of O.J. Simpson, who just happened to be in the Orange Bowl, doing *Monday Night Football* for ABC. We'd gotten wind that O.J. hadn't been too kind to the Bears in weeks past, or to Wally. Simpson apparently listed the great running backs on one telecast, and he left out Payton, which is unbelievable if O.J. intended it.

Anyway, we were down 38–24 and Ditka sent in two straight passing plays with Dennis Gentry. I couldn't understand it. To make a long story short, I had a discussion with Ditka about it.

"What did I tell you to call?" he asked, as if I didn't know.

"Let's get Wally his hundred yards," I said.

"Oh, well, how many does he need?" Ditka said.

We ran the ball, and Wally got his hundred yards, even though he'd hardly been called on during the first half. I'm not one to surrender, no matter what, but to me, it wasn't that important, trying to pull a miracle out of the bag at that point. The game wasn't that important. What was important was Wally getting his record. Show the man a little respect. I don't know if Wally appreciated what I did, but I do know I appreciate him.

I can't say the same about film sessions. At this level, the game is so much more mental than physical. Besides, the way I see, which isn't good, those films aren't going to help me that much. They're taken from upstairs, a completely different angle from the one you view the game, at field level. It's almost as though the films you watch on Monday are of a completely different game from the one you played on Sunday.

They have some value. You should watch the reel of your next opponent in blitz situations, then the reel for third-down coverages. Otherwise, a quarterback has it all written down for him, what the other team's tendencies are. You've got the printouts. They'll do this on first and 10 inside their 50-yard line, or this if you get inside their 20. For a lineman who is working one-on-one against another guy, a lot of film might help. But a quarterback has to grasp what's happening, or what might happen, on the entire field.

I always remember one of the first lessons a coach taught me as a kid. If you don't know the answer to something you see out there, react like a football player. *React.* That's what football is about—*instincts.* It's not as difficult as it's made out to be, and if you spend all your time behind the projector during the week, you can get so wrapped up in formations and such that you get vapor lock on Sunday.

Wait a minute! you'll say to yourself coming out of a huddle. *They aren't lined up the way they were in the films!* Then what? Then it's too late, unless you can react, unless you have the proper instincts. You can't teach instinct, especially in a dark room. You'll learn more in those five seconds between when you break the huddle and when you call the signals than you will in five days of watching films. That's when you see what the other team is doing to you, and when you decide what you can do to them. Just by looking. By reacting. They're doing something different? Okay, so we'll do something different.

I've got to thank Brigham Young for a lot of my success. By playing that offense, with such an emphasis on throwing, I came into the NFL a lot more prepared than a lot of other college quarterbacks. I knew how to read defenses and, more important, I knew how to improvise, to execute. In college, every week was something new. Teams always played us differently. In the pros, the defenses are actually a lot more predictable than in college. Still, unless the other team does in the game exactly what it did in the films, you're on your own to some extent.

You can get a good indication of what the other team has

in mind by the front three or four linemen. Most teams will tie their pass coverage to the way they set up, but not all. Some teams won't tip their hand. So, I also look at the eyes of the defensive backs as soon as I get out of the huddle and come to the line of scrimmage. The eyes never lie. If a defensive back is going to cover somebody, he'll be looking at him. You can learn a lot by looking at who the other team is looking at. I've called plays on that hunch alone—the eyes of an opposing defensive back. You can also smell a blitz by how deep they're positioned. The more you play, the more you pick up, the more repetition will help you.

Also, remember that with everything that goes on out there, someone is bound to make a mistake. Just hope it isn't your team. You spend all that time preparing for a big game, and still someone will blow an assignment. Look what happened in our playoff game against the Giants. The cornerback blitzed. The free safety went over to cover our wideout. But the strong safety forgot to cover Tim Wrightman, and he was wide open for a big gain. These things happen, especially when everybody depends on one another.

I'm not a whole lot smarter than any other quarterback in the NFL. I still make my stupid plays; I still throw my interceptions, which is the worst possible thing for a quarterback. I'd rather eat the ball than throw it into another guy's hands, but so would we all, and we still have those times when we screw up. I usually know right away when I've thrown an interception; I get so mad I start running right at the guy who's going to pick it off. A rotten feeling. When you're in trouble, some quarterbacks will throw it away out-of-bounds; others will heave it wild on the field. I always try to make a play if at all possible, but some days, you get burned. That's all there is to it.

I'm six-foot-one, which is supposed to mean I'm too small. At least that was the rap on me. If I were six-three, just so I could see a little better over those behemoths on the line, see through the lanes, I'd be illegal. If I were six-five or six-six, I'd not only be a Greek god, I'd probably be in the NBA, making a better living shooting the hoops and not getting abused every Sunday. I always loved baseball, especially growing up near San Francisco and Willie Mays. I could handle hockey, too, because that looks like fun. Except, whenever I put skates on, my feet get awfully sore. Must be all those bones I've broken.

What else could I be doing if I wasn't doing what I'm doing? Definitely not boxing. Those poor guys have to run for five months before every fight. No way. Wrestling? Sorry, I never did like the idea of touching another man in his private property. Soccer? Same thing as boxing. Too much running. I swore off that at an early age. Bowling I just swore at, because I could never knock down that last pin.

So, here I am, a small quarterback with not much speed and not much vision. Some of my critics don't think I have much of an arm, either, although I feel I've got as good a release as anybody in the game. I first realized I had a good arm when I started throwing rocks at other kids. But I throw more ducks now than I used to, and fewer spirals, because, I think, of the footballs. They keep bringing new ones into the game, sometimes as many as sixteen or twenty, and although they say they rub them down, they're too slippery for me. I have fairly small hands, and I just can't grab the thing as well as some of the other guys in the NFL. Hell, I shook hands with Ken O'Brien of the Jets and I thought he was an orangutan. Huge paws on that dude.

But, just like I don't fear pain anymore, I'm not afraid to shake it up once in a while and do something bizarre. In college, every Friday before a Saturday game, I'd switch off and throw with my left arm for an hour. That not only saved my right arm, but it gave me confidence with my left. I've thrown with my left for 50 yards in practice, and I've thrown with my left in games, college and pro, when in severe heat.

Whatever it takes. Shovel passes, southpaw passes. Why don't more quarterbacks do that? I don't know, maybe they're afraid to take chances. But, no guts, no glory.

When I was also punting in college, there was a game against Hawaii when the center snapped the ball over my head. I scrambled after it—the ball, not my head—spun to my left, then drop-kicked it with my left foot, about 30 yards to their 1. If I'd have straightened up to kick with my right foot, my real kicking foot, I'd have been smothered. Whenever I go back to Hawaii, people still remind me of that. What do they call it? Grace under pressure?

Something like that keeps everybody alert, and, besides, it's entertaining—if it works. Our offense on the Bears would be a little boring without me, if I do say so myself. We're still run-oriented, but not as much as we used to be. Other teams know they should expect anything and everything now, though I'd love to throw 30 to 35 times a game instead of what we average now, which is maybe 20. It's tough to develop any rhythm that way, especially when you're throwing in third-down situations. It's a lot easier to throw on first, but we're still getting there.

Under Bill Walsh, the San Francisco 49ers have established a great offense for Joe Montana, whose athletic ability just adds another dimension. So does Roger Craig's, who's really an extra receiver, even though he's a running back. It would be interesting being in Dan Marino's shoes, too. He gets to fire about 45 times a week for Miami. He's a pure thrower, although he doesn't do a lot of the other things. He doesn't have to. I'd love to see how Marino would do on our offense. He wouldn't pile up those fancy stats he gets with the Dolphins, that's for sure.

Buddy Ryan, our defensive coach before he went to Philadelphia as head man, always said that the guys who give him the most trouble are the quarterbacks who move around, who get outside. Marino did that against us in 1985, and it surprised us. I'd prefer to throw instead of run, but I like to keep them guessing best of all. If it's between having to thread a needle or pick an opening to run for 30 yards, there's no percentage there. Run. Our coaches have told me to slide or go out of bounds to play it safe, but most of the times you're going to get hit anyway, so you might as well get hit while getting an extra yard or two. It only hurts for a little while, unless they find your kidney while they're trying to kill you. The quarterback is the one player nobody guards, but that doesn't mean they don't want a piece of you. The big rap on most quarterbacks is that we're too fragile, but I don't buy it. A lot of guys in pro football—Montana, Danny White—will throw a block if they get a chance. I'm not the only one. We're tougher than you think. Even Joe Theismann, the prettiest of them all, has taken his lumps. That Monday night game in 1985 when he broke his leg against the Giants was one of the most grotesque things I've ever seen.

I do carry myself like a bit of a hot dog sometimes, I admit. I'm not afraid of giving lip to some guy who's twice my size. I'm also not afraid to speak up to the coach when I don't like something, and I think that's part of what makes your teammates regard you as a leader. I don't think my teammates feel I'm too abrasive or cocky when I lash out at them, or Ditka, or anybody else when I get a little hot. In the end, they know all I want to do is win. They also should know that nobody gets madder at myself than me. Besides, it isn't all that grim in the huddle. You have some great laughs, especially when you're winning.

"Did you see me flatten that guy?" Kurt Becker will ask me.

"No, but I did see you spit on him," I'll answer.

The Los Angeles Raiders, whom I've mentioned as a dream team, let their quarterbacks call their own plays a lot more than most places, including Chicago. Ditka still calls most of our plays, although I've audibilized, or changed up on the line of scrimmage, more and more in the last couple of years. I don't call an audible just to call an audible, though. The coaches know what they're doing. At least, they should. One of our assistant coaches, Ed Hughes, is an excellent offensive mind. That's why they're paid to be there. I just wish we weren't quite so structured and so complicated as we are on the Bears. There are so many chances for breakdowns when Ditka gets in one of his Einstein moods, but the longer this team is together, the smoother things will run.

Especially if I can manage to stay healthy for an entire season. I have an inkling what caused my downfall in 1984. A few nights before we played the Raiders, the Bears had our Halloween party. I dressed up like Father Mulcahy in *M*A*S*H*. The priest's collar, the cross, the whole bit. I even had a "Bible" with me, except that when I opened it to read a prayer to my teammates, there were a bunch of pictures of naked women.

I thought it was pretty funny, pretty harmless. Until the next game, when I got my lacerated kidney. I think the Man Upstairs was telling me something, and I don't mean Michael McCaskey. What I'd done at the Halloween party was sacrilegeous. I'll never do it again. If I ever wear another collar, I'll make sure it's dirty. Then, people will think I'm disguised as a sportswriter.

ELEVEN

Growing Up . . . and Away

I was born to be a hellion. I was tough on other children, tough on my parents, and fairly tough on myself.

Like when I was six. I was putting myself to good use one day, trying to untie a lace on my gun holster. I was sort of slumped over, using a fork. The fork slipped and went crashing into my right eye. I knew I'd screwed up badly, because I was bawling. No blood, just a lot of tears. I washed the fork off, then went back to just sit quietly in a chair, afraid to tell my mother, Roberta.

My father, Jim, was at work at the time, and he had our family's only car. I was scared. So I waited. Waited for six hours before I told my mom, and we finally made it to the hospital, a place I didn't care for then any more than I care for now.

I had severed the retina, and the doctors told my parents they couldn't save the eye. Nobody told me that, but being a fine student, even at that age, I didn't have to be told. I remember wondering whether I'd go blind. This fear apparently didn't affect my appetite, because I ate dinner before I went to the hospital. That delayed the operation until the next morning. Can't have surgery on your eye if you have something in your stomach, I guess.

I don't remember a whole lot about what followed, except that they tied me to a bed for a week, so I wouldn't scratch the eye, which itched like hell. There are Monday mornings now when I wish I could be tied to a bed, but when you're six with a patch over your eye, that's not a comfortable way to be. My equilibrium was screwed up, as if I had sipped too many beverages, and many times the nurses would come in and find me squirming all over the place, trying to bend around somehow to scratch the thing with my knee.

It didn't take me long to make a brat of myself. When I was moved to a wheelchair, I started cruising around the halls. I hung out—if you could use that term—with this poor kid in an oxygen tent. There was another kid in there who would pick on the kid in the oxygen tent. I didn't appreciate that, so whenever it came time for meals, I'd rev up my wheelchair, whiz on by the kid who was picking on my friend in the oxygen bubble, and steal his food. We put an end to that abuse. I was always for the underdog.

Pretty soon, a few of us in the same wing got hold of a Whiffle ball and bat and started having our very own games to pass the time. I hit the ball out of the window one morning, and went out looking for it. I don't know how many stories up we were, but when the nurse on duty showed up, seeing me climbing around the roof of the hospital with a patch on my eye, after bolting from the wheelchair . . . well, she about needed to take over my bed. I thought she was going to have a heart attack.

"What are you doing out there, young man!! What are you doing out there? Come back. Come back this minute!"

I wore a patch a long while after I got out of the hospital. A couple of months, at least. It hurt like hell, but my parents did all the worrying. My aggravation started when they took the patch off. My eyesight was weak and blurry. I could hardly see at all. Worse than that, though, I had to wear these glasses with the Coke-bottle lenses. You can figure out how well that went over with the other kids. That must have been right around when I learned how to fight. I was always fighting.

The right eye has gradually gotten better over the years. They told me I'd never be able to use it again, but I fooled 'em. Course, if I had two eyes like the right one, I'd never be a quarterback. Either that, or I'd have to hand off a lot. I have problems making out details sometimes from a distance, which, of course, is the reason I occasionally throw a ball to a man with the wrong color uniform. That's the worst drawback, next to glancing over to the sidelines every so often and seeing three Ditkas. It's a good thing I didn't also stick a fork in my ear. Then I might be *hearing* three Ditkas, too. Anyway, that's why I wear sunglasses whenever possible. Not because I'm trying to be cool. Because my right eye is still very sensitive, especially to bright lights. It is most comfortable where it's dark, such as a bar or a bedroom.

All of this business with my eye happened in San Jose, California. I was born in Jersey City, New Jersey, but don't remember anything about it. My parents actually met in Chicago, when they were both in the service. My older brother, Mike, was born in Chicago. Then we moved to Jersey City, then moved again to California when I was three.

My first school there was Hellyer Elementary, which was fitting. Hellyer. Hellion. I majored in recess and minored in dodgeball. I particularly enjoyed throwing things at moving objects, especially if those objects were heads of classmates I didn't care for. I was very scrawny then, which is another reason why I probably was always getting into fights. I was also very hyperactive, and bored by doing things I had no use for. That still holds today.

In kindergarten, I started learning the fine art of being a

brat. Early in life, early in the morning. During the flag salute, I would grab some thumbtacks and sneak underneath a desk. There, I'd take the tacks and stick them in the fat rear end of this Hawaiian kid, who never did make it through the Pledge of Allegiance without screaming. I just wanted to let some of the air out of that balloon.

I kept trying to convince my teacher that the fat Hawaiian kid was just very patriotic, that he couldn't say the flag salute without getting all emotional. She didn't buy it, for reasons I could never understand. So, the principal would be called in and he'd push me against the wall. Then, they'd call my mom, and she'd come in. Then they'd call the Hawaiian kid's fat Hawaiian mother, and they'd all ask for an apology. My mother handled that. I still haven't said I'm sorry.

That sort of thing helped get me through the day. Later on, I moved on to bigger and better things, like throwing firecrackers during shop class. At Sylvandale Junior High School, I was constantly getting punished, then expelled for a couple of days at a time. They never put me back a grade for two reasons. One—and don't ask me why—my grades weren't that bad. Two, they wanted to get me the hell out of there before I blew the place up. Maybe that's why I got good grades, come to think of it.

When I was twelve, I got kicked off the baseball team for getting caught smoking cigarettes. Not only was my dad the coach, but they were *his* cigarettes. I'd steal them, then go to the orchards to light up, or the nearby gas station, where I became friendly with the bums. If it weren't for sports, that's where I'd probably be today. Hanging around the gas station, smoking cigarettes with my fellow bums.

But, fortunately, I really got into athletics. I especially enjoyed baseball and football. I started organized football when I was ten. They had a simple way to figure out who'd be a quarterback. They lined everybody up, and whoever threw the ball farthest was it. I was it, even though I was skinny, with knock-knees and bad eyesight. At Andrew Hill High School, I started in freshman ball, then was with the varsity my sophomore year, too, before we moved to Utah. I never played junior varsity. I was getting the idea then that I was pretty decent. I was getting pretty thirsty, too. I remember this Little League picnic when I was only thirteen. We were supposed to play the parents, and I got my hands on some champagne, so I decided to have a few cocktails to celebrate the event. I overserved myself, so when the game started, there I was out in left field, puking. I was hoping nobody would hit the ball to me so I wouldn't have to run. I was in enough pain as it was. I have disliked champagne ever since. I might have a couple of glasses on New Year's Eve; I know I had a couple when Nance and I got married. But I still remember that day in left field, when I was thirteen, the first time I got drunk.

That's just about when the heat was really on for me to become a better citizen. About eighth grade. I was forever being warned by teachers, principals, or the police, when necessary, about staying out of trouble. My parents let me have it, too. I was punished regularly and deserved it. Not just my father, either. Roberta could also wield a mean broomstick.

I did reform briefly, but reverted to my old form when we moved to Roy, Utah. Another transfer for my dad, and one that I wasn't too thrilled about. Mike, my older brother by eleven months, was allowed to stay in California to finish school. I wanted to, also, and the coaches at Andrew Hill even offered to put me up because they wanted me to keep playing football there. My parents wanted to keep me under their thumb, and I guess I can't blame them. If I'd have stayed in California, with its life-style, I might have really gone wild.

We never had a lot of money. In San Jose, we lived in a neighborhood with a lot of black kids, and we always got along. I never really lacked anything, but I do remember that most of the children my age were out and about all the time. My parents were a lot stricter, and maybe that's where I got this thing about challenging authority every so often. I got physical with a couple of teachers, slapping them, and that wasn't real smart. Then, my parents would find out and beat the crap out of me.

I had this one stretch of vandalism in junior high school. My buddy's dad was a janitor and we got a key to the building. Late at night, we'd slip in and raise a little havoc. He'd break TV sets, kick in movie projectors, shatter blackboards, whatever. I was the graffiti expert. When we got caught—naturally, we got caught—my punishment was cleaning off all the graffiti. I can tell you this: It's a lot easier to apply graffiti than get rid of it.

Mike, my goody-goody brother, went with us on a couple of these search-and-destroy missions, but I never told on him. What's the difference? What's the use? The last time he came over to our house not long ago, we were alone once and he asked me why I never snitched on him. That's what I told him. What's the use? My buddy and I were in trouble; why make it three?

By the time I got to Roy, I was an accomplished hellion, but a pretty good football player, too. I'd played one year of varsity in California, and didn't arrive at Roy High School until they were already having two-a-day practices during the summer. I sat in the car one day, watching their two quarterbacks. I said to myself, If I can't beat out those two guys, I'm quitting football. I was the third-team quarterback for the first couple of weeks. Then came our first scrimmage, from the wishbone formation. The No. 1 quarterback had the first-team offense against the second-team defense. The No. 2 quarterback had the second-team offense against the third-team defense. I had the third-team offense against the first-team defense, and we scored a bunch. I wound up starting the first game, and all the rest, too. We went 11–1 my junior year before losing in the state semifinals. My senior year, we were 8–2 and lost in the quarterfinal of the tournament.

I made some good friends, mostly guys who played sports like me, and liked to have a few laughs. I also had a girlfriend here and there, too. One in particular was helpful. She'd save all her English papers, then type them over and give them to me. The teacher knew what was going on, but that might have been my first experience with preferential treatment for athletes. My girlfriend would get B's and C's on her papers, and I'd get A's. That upset her a bit. I couldn't cheat on oral exams. But I got by with some decent grades, all the while thinking more and more about making sports my occupation, if at all possible.

I had played varsity football and baseball in my sophomore year at Andrew Hill, then all three sports—football, baseball, and basketball—for my junior and senior years after coming to Utah. When it was time to start thinking about college, a lot of the local schools were chasing me. Utah State, for one, offered me a basketball scholarship, but I didn't like the future there. There weren't too many six-foot white guards running around then, especially ones who couldn't dunk.

I was Catholic, and still am, so naturally I had this fantasy about going to Notre Dame. When you're growing up, watching TV on Sunday mornings, it was either Notre Dame highlights from the day before or a religious program. I took Notre Dame. I also thought about trying Grambling, so I maybe could be the only white guy in the backfield. I figured I needed to work on my speed; if I went to Grambling, maybe a little would rub off on me.

I took a recruiting trip to Nebraska. I had a good time, and a few beverages, but it was a waste. I wanted to throw the ball in college, and Nebraska was pretty much run-oriented. I considered Boise State, because I'd never been to Idaho. Maybe I could major in football and minor in potatoes. Talked with Mike White, now the Illinois coach, who was then at California–Berkeley. Oklahoma State was in there somewhere, too. Tom Lasorda, the manager of the Los Angeles Dodgers, even called. He was friends with one of the coaches at Utah State. Lasorda, who'd managed there for years for the Dodgers' farm team in Ogden, Utah, was talking about a baseball career for me, which was also appealing. Meanwhile, the people from Utah State were telling me how strange I might feel at another place I was seriously considering: Brigham Young University. Were they ever telling the truth.

Finally, it came down to the day of decision. There were three coaches over at our house in Roy. One from Las Vegas–Nevada, one from Utah State, one from Brigham Young. Each of them thought he was the one. I had to declare, and I did. "I think I'll be a Cougar," I said. I was going to Brigham Young, on a full ride. My parents were elated.

I often wonder if that was the last time I made them really happy. They had really pushed and pushed for Brigham Young. There was no pressure on me to succeed in sports earlier in my childhood. Nothing like that. My dad was supportive, but he didn't push. Of course, he didn't have to. That's all I ever wanted to do, play sports.

But they did push for Brigham Young; in the end, I went there for their sake. When we were sitting around the kitchen table, with me about to make my big decision, I could see how uptight they were. It was like, wherever I went on a recruiting trip, I liked for a day or two. I was always leaning toward the last place I went, or so it seemed. My parents could never figure me out. I can't figure them out, either. I've got my older brother, Mike, a younger brother, Danny, and three sisters, Robin, Linda, and Stacy. They've all stayed pretty close to home, geographically and emotionally, but not me. I'm here in Chicago, playing football, and I can't say that I'm at all tight with my parents.

It's as though, when I was a kid, I could do nothing wrong

with them on the athletic field, and nothing right off it. People hear that and ask whether I didn't get my full tank of love. I'm not sure it was that, because I don't feel any hatred for them now. I care about them. I love them.

But I can't stand to go back to Utah to see them, and I make every effort to avoid it, because whenever I do wind up there, I have a miserable time. We start fighting about little things, and before you know it, we're at each other's throats. I have no desire to have them come to Chicago, either, and most of the reason is the way they treat Nancy.

I don't know why they act like they do, but they were mad when I got married to her and they've been cold to her ever since. Maybe they look at her as the one who took me away from them. Well, isn't that normal? Isn't that the way it's supposed to be? You get married to the woman you love, you start your own life, you build your own family, and so on. That doesn't mean you don't have any use for your parents.

But, I'm not going to put up with the way they act toward Nancy. She sends them packages of pictures, writes them letters, and then when they call, they never even thank her. The first thing they say if she answers the phone is, "Where's Jim?" They have nothing to say to Nancy, and if it bothers her, it bothers me even worse. If they want to blame me for pulling away from them, fine. But I wish they'd check the mirror once in a while.

My dad and mom are a little too loud, for one thing. If they want to share in what I've done as a football player, that's fine. But I don't care for them being so pushy. My dad showed up in San Francisco for our game two years ago, asking for tickets like he always does at the last minute. Then he bumped into Ed McCaskey, the chairman of the board of the Bears, and wound up asking for McCaskey's necktie. As bold as I am, I know you can't do things like that. I'm not too keen on him showing up with his Jim McMahon T-shirt on, either, the one with a huge 9 on the back. That's not being proud. That's being overly proud.

They sometimes live in a dream world, too, thinking that NFL players fly their parents all over the country to see games. They showed up in Tampa Bay a couple of years ago, made a point of telling me how they had paid their own way, then demanded tickets and demanded that I go out to dinner with them Saturday night before the game. Just like that. Well, they got their tickets, but I didn't go to dinner with them. I didn't go to dinner at all that night. I saw them for ten minutes.

It was the same thing for the Super Bowl. They called ahead wanting seven tickets. I told them I had only five left because they called so late. They said they had to have seven for them and friends. We got into a big fight, and they started crying and hung up; then my brother Mike calls to referee. "What's wrong with you and Pop?" he'll say. They got their seven tickets, but we didn't spend any time together in New Orleans. After the game, they came up to my room for maybe five or ten minutes, then just took off for the big team party downstairs.

I told them I didn't want to go. Then I just poked my head in a while later. Someone said my dad saw me walking around, and he just turned around and walked the other way. He thought I'd lied to him. I told him I wasn't going to the party, and then I showed up. It's always something.

But, mostly it's the way they are with Nancy. I suppose they would have been the same way with anybody I married. They took part in everything with me, especially in college, and now they don't have much of a part at all. They could have it if they weren't so stubborn and so childish, but the ball's in their court. I've tried to be good to them, but until they're good to Nancy, all bets are off.

I don't know what they really think of me anymore. At least when I was growing up, and they made me do a week of washing dishes—the one thing I absolutely hated—I knew that they were mad, that they were punishing me. And when they got their Irish up and let me have it with the strap, I knew. But I don't have a handle on their feelings now, except they probably think I've gotten a big head, that I've made a lot of money, that I don't need them anymore. I can imagine some of the things they say about their jerk son and his wife.

Again, I can't lay this all on a really unhappy childhood or anything like that. I had my moments. I didn't exactly run away from home, but there were times when I'd just take off and stay at a friend's house without them knowing. Strangely enough, I got along with everybody else's parents better than my own. I always used to have fun with parents of the girls I took out. Even when I stopped dating their daughters, I would drop over to see the parents.

But, here I am and I don't even feel comfortable around my own parents. I've tried to talk to them, but it does no good. Sooner or later, we'll start screaming at each other. Then, click. Then we won't talk for weeks. That big blowup about tickets before the Super Bowl really bugged me. And then Nancy saw that I was affected, and she started crying. I don't need it. I can't take it. It's not right, but that's the way it is.

If they needed help of any kind, I would help, but they don't. I'd still like to take care of them in some way when I finally become financially secure, but they aren't hurting. We never had a bunch of money lying around, like I said, but they're okay. They take their trips, they have their fun. They just don't have much of it with Nancy and me, which is a shame, but it doesn't look like it's going to change.

I suppose I'm the guilty one because I'm the only one of the children who didn't stay close to home. I suppose I'm the black sheep, the ungrateful one, in their minds. If I had no feeling for my parents, then I wouldn't let this thing with them bother me. But it does.

Last Christmas, there were no gifts from us to them, or them to us. No telephone calls either. Then, weeks later, my dad telephoned for his Super Bowl tickets. After insulting Nancy, he tore into me.

"I can't believe my son didn't even call me on Christmas," he said.

"We're always calling you," I said. "Why don't *you* call *us* once in a while just to say hello? Why didn't you call us on Christmas?"

"Because, Jim, you changed your phone number." My father's voice started to crack. "We didn't know how to get ahold of you."

"I have the same number now that I had then," I said. "And you got ahold of me for Super Bowl tickets."

It's brutal. But, it's their move. I've had some great times in the past with my parents, my brothers and sisters. I'd like to have more in the future. There's one thing I've got to get ironed out, though. If Jim and Roberta McMahon love me as much as they say they do, why can't they show some love for the woman I love?

TWELVE

Off to Disneyland

Having given my parents their wish, I went tripping off to Disneyland, otherwise known as Brigham Young University, in the summer of 1977. I call it Disneyland because it's an unreal world out there in Provo, Utah. Most of the people are Mormons, and most of them aren't normal, as I see it.

But before I get into all my ups and downs there, I should clear one thing up. I think I would have become an NFL quarterback no matter where I went to college. Going to Brigham Young, though, helped me make it to the pros a whole lot. I learned about people at BY *Who*, even if it was one of the happiest moments of my life when I got out of there.

Strangely enough, when I left home for college, I thought the same thing, that I'd finally been set free. Well, I had some good times at Brigham Young, but I also had to deal with some heavy hypocrisy. When you go there, you sign a paper promising to abide by the codes of the Mormon religion: no alcohol, smoking, etc. Yet, the same environment that claims to have this superior life-style puts up with some of the same things—drugs, booze, cheating—that you see at some of the schools where you don't have to give a blood oath about leading a moral life.

Plus, you get the idea there that Mormons are the chosen people while everybody else is inferior, an outsider to the human race. I have some great friends who are Mormons. My wife, Nancy, is Mormon. But I don't believe in that business about me being better than you. Maybe that goes back to San Jose, when we were one of only three or four white families on our block. I didn't check a kid's color or background before I played catch with him. You know, live and let live.

But, I went to Brigham Young to play football. I make no bones about it. And I played football. Not much of it my freshman year, when I was almost exclusively a punter. Gifford Nielson, the No. 1 quarterback, went down with an injury in the fourth game of the season, against Oregon State. I came in and my first pass was tipped and picked off by Bubba Baker. Modest beginnings, to be sure. I wound up the year with ten completions in sixteen attempts and one touchdown, against Texas–El Paso in our last game.

I didn't get into much trouble my freshman season. I met Nancy late in the year, then decided I had to have wheels. You didn't get any money under the table at BYU, that's for sure, so I took out a loan for two thousand dollars. My dad cosigned for it, and I wound up in a grand old Duster with a green top and green interior. The seats were ripped, so you always left the car with some pillow all over your pants, but it ran. In the summer, I was also driving a truck as a job. I preferred my Duster, ripped seats and all.

Nielson was gone my sophomore year, drafted by the Houston Oilers. So was Doug Scovil, one of our assistant coaches, who left to join the Bears. The new offensive coordinator was Wally English, who was a beauty. If I learned a lot about football from some of the rest of the staff, all I learned from English was how to be wishy-washy, how to be wrong.

I remember one incident in practice involving Marc Wilson, who was supposed to be the next Mormon superman. The play was designed for Wilson to hit the tight end, but he'd roll out and throw it to the wideout, time and again. English went crazy. Then I'd go in there with the same instructions and do the same thing—I'd throw to the wideout instead of the tight end. English went crazy again. Only difference was, I went crazy back at him.

"The bleeping tight end isn't open!" I screamed at English. "You can't throw to him, because the play doesn't work! So buzz off!"

When we went into the huddle, the guys were laughing like hell. Who is this crazy SOB of a sophomore telling this coach off? As it turned out, English checked the film of the drill that night and realized he was wrong. The tight end had been covered. He apologized to me the next day. I don't know if anybody lost respect for Wilson that day because he kept his mouth shut, but I figure they realized for maybe the first time that they had a dude on their hands who *was* going to speak his piece. Me.

Wilson was No. 1 at the start of my sophomore year. He got hurt in the third game, I went in, then he returned a week later, but was struggling. We were 3–2 and trailing a winless Oregon team 16–3 when LaVell Edwards, our head coach, pulled Wilson in the third quarter and put me in. I went 10 for 19 for 204 yards and one touchdown and we won 17–16. A few days later, Edwards said, "McMahon is now our number one quarterback."

I started the next four games, including a 24-for-36 day against Wyoming, before I had to sit out a game in Hawaii because of tendinitis in my left knee. Wilson started. Fine, I thought. We're the Western Athletic Conference champions, we're going to the Holiday Bowl in San Diego against Navy soon, I'll get healed and get ready to start the game. Right? I will start the Holiday Bowl, won't I? "Don't worry," said LaVell, "you'll start the Holiday Bowl game."

Well, I didn't start the Holiday Bowl game. I was practicing with the first team all week when, one afternoon, English came up to me.

"Marc is starting against Navy," he said.

I blew up. In the first place, I didn't like the idea of LaVell lying to me. And I didn't like the idea of him sending his flunky, Wally English, to tell me the bad news, either. I gave English a piece of my mind; then I went to find Edwards. We wound up at poolside. I made a few waves.

"You told me in Hawaii, even though I was hurt, that I'd play here in San Diego," I screamed.

"I never would say a thing like that," Edwards said.

"You're a liar," I informed him. "I've had enough of Brigham Young. I'm gonna look to get out of this place."

I was serious, too, until Brent Pratley took me under his wing. Pratley was the new team doctor, a regular guy, a normal Mormon who became like a surrogate father to me in years to come. He was always there when I needed him, particularly when my Duster broke down, which was fairly often. Pratley had five cars, including a Mercedes, a Porsche, and a Cadillac. Brent let me take a spin in his machines, but the spies at BYU always knew.

There was a reserved parking spot for the team doctor by the athletic compound, and somehow, whenever I parked there, even though it was in Brent's car, there was a ticket waiting when I arrived back. The explanation was that the place belonged to the doctor's car only if the doctor was driving it. Not if I was driving it. I told you they made a lot of sense at BYU.

Brent Pratley made a lot of sense, though, at first over my

objections. He reminded me that I'd had a pretty good year, even with the Holiday Bowl business. I'd made the All-Western Athletic Conference team as a sophomore, the first quarterback to do that. I was at the perfect place to throw the ball. I was at the perfect place to shoot for the Heisman Trophy, which goes to the best college football player of the year. (I'd announced my intentions to do that, which also must have endeared me to the folks at BYU.)

"You're right, Brent," I said one afternoon in his office. "I should stay, if for no other reason than to shove it to these people."

Not so fast. Scovil returned for 1979, and the first words out of his mouth were, "We have to get Marc Wilson back to form." Wonderful. Scovil hadn't liked me before he left, partly, I think, because I was also playing baseball. I had a feeling they'd give me a hard time and I didn't help myself by not rehabilitating my knee the way I could have. It was hurting, Wilson played and led BYU to an 11–0 record, and I red-shirted. I wanted to keep that year of eligibility; I didn't want to waste it on the sidelines, watching, wondering about my knee. Wilson had an outstanding season. I didn't like the inactivity, but I was glad in the end that I stuck it out.

The next season, 1980, began in heat but ended well. I missed the mile run at the start of camp because I attended a hellacious wedding party the night before. Edwards was furious and so was Scovil, who was known to keep a bottle tucked away in his desk. Then everybody joined in, getting on my back, when we lost to New Mexico 25–21 in our opener. I was 11 for 25 and paying for a summer of relaxation, beverages, and golf.

Fortunately, I got it together. We won 11 straight after that, some by unbelievable scores: 52 points against Wyoming, 70 against Utah State, 83 against Texas–El Paso. I wound up with 47 touchdown passes, an NCAA season's record, for 4,571 yards, also a record. We also went to the Holiday Bowl again, and this time I played. Played maybe the game of my life.

I was terrible for a while in that game. We all were, and Southern Methodist, our opponent in San Diego, was thrashing us with Craig James and Eric Dickerson. We trailed 38–19 midway in the fourth quarter. We were moving the ball a bit on one series, but came up short on fourth down. LaVell sent the punting team in. I told our guys to huddle up. One of the guys told me we couldn't huddle up, the coach was sending in the punting team.

"Huddle up!!" I repeated. LaVell and Scovil just looked at each other on the sidelines. They didn't know what to make of me. I wasn't going to quit. They should have figured that out right then. We went on to score, but we missed the conversion, and trailed 38–25.

James came right back to score for SMU, making it 45–25 with 4:07 left. It was time to get serious. I threw a touchdown pass. We tried an onside kick and got it. We scored again. We tried another onside kick and didn't get it, but SMU had the ball for three downs and we stopped them. They tried to punt, but our Bill Schoepflin blocked it. We had the ball. I threw two incompletions, and so we were at their 46-yard line with three seconds left on the clock.

It was time for our "Hail Mary," or "Save the Game," pass play that we'd practiced a bit. Basically, it was: everybody go deep and if you get close to the ball, catch it. I dropped back about 10 yards to give my guys time, then I threw it as high as I could, as far as I could. Clay Brown, our tight end, had five guys around him about midway in the end zone. Time had expired.

But Clay Brown got close to the ball, and caught the ball. Touchdown. We won 46–45. I looked over at LaVell and Scovil. They were shocked. SMU was shocked. The fans were shocked. We were delirious in the locker room afterward. Some people were calling it the most exciting bowl game ever. It was wild. The Cougars went from dead meat to the talk of the country.

I finished with 446 yards passing, and 230 of them must have been in the fourth quarter. I stayed on the West Coast after that and drove up to Nancy's house with her. I was a lot more at ease now, figuring that maybe the folks at BYU would like me a little better after that game.

They did and they didn't. I threw for 30 touchdowns in my senior year, when I missed two games because of my left knee problems again. I blew it out in Colorado. I had almost 300 yards in the first half, then collapsed on the first series of the third quarter. The fans cheered, as if to say, "That's what we do to cocky quarterbacks around here." I pointed to the scoreboard, as if to say, "That's what we do to sorry football teams." We won 41–20.

It was a weird year. In one game, against Air Force, they didn't rush anybody to guard against the pass. All eleven of their players lay back, protecting against screens, bombs, whatever. We killed them, and I had 28 completions in 39 attempts. Then in our last game, against our traditional rival Utah, I cracked three vertebrae. The pain was killing me, but I continued to play. With four minutes left in a game we'd win 56–28, I had 565 yards passing. The BYU record was 571, by Wilson. I'd have loved to break it, but they took me out. Wilson, after all, was a Mormon. Couldn't let a cocky Catholic kid break his record.

I traveled around doing a bunch of banquets that winter, all the while needing only nineteen hours to get my diploma. But I never finished. After football was done, they just happened to discover that I'd been seen drinking and chewing tobacco around campus. After my being around there five years, they just happened to see me now that my football eligibility was done. They said good-bye but I could come back to finish my classes later on sometime. I said good-bye, I'm never coming back.

I don't imagine they're too thrilled back at BYU to call me an alum. They probably don't mind all the publicity they got while I was there, or all the tickets they sold, but the fact that I wasn't a model citizen didn't excite them. They never bothered to push me much for the Heisman Trophy, which I never won. George Rogers got it my junior year; Marcus Allen my senior year. I got the handshake and the boot.

I did some strange things, had some strange jobs, and met all sorts of people while doing time in Provo.

Probably the craziest maneuver I pulled was in Hawaii my junior year. I came back to the hotel one night, after a few beverages, and decided I'd drop in on the twenty-third floor from my room on the twenty-fourth floor. Nothing unusual about that, except I bypassed the elevator. I went out on our patio, lowered myself to where I was grabbing the ledge, then swung my body back and forth until I let go while I was swinging toward the building. I had a fine landing, on the patio below mine, but there was nobody home. So I went back up to my room the same way, climbing up from patio to patio.

"You're crazy," said Pluto, who was taking this all in. I couldn't argue with him. When I woke up the next morning, vaguely recollecting what I'd done, I went outside on the patio and looked down below. Put it this way: If I'd have slipped, if I hadn't had such a quiet landing, I wouldn't be writing this book.

Some of my other brushes with trouble were more routine. I was caught drinking beer on the golf course during the summer, put on probation; caught chewing tobacco, put on probation; caught with beer in my room, put on probation. You get the idea. If I hadn't played football, I wouldn't have lasted, I don't think. Maybe they would have cared less if I had been just another student. Maybe they wouldn't have. I know I always seemed to be under the microscope. I would go to a party in Ogden one night, and the next day, LaVell would know about it at practice. I don't know how. Somebody must have been out to get me. I learned to trust fewer and fewer people there, including LaVell, who I basically like, who I played a lot of golf with. He always told me, if you have to have your beers, Jim, do it discreetly. LaVell wasn't a bad guy, but he did lie to me that one time. I don't forget that.

I met some good folks, like Brent Pratley and his family, who gave me my first suit. Black pin-striped. Like Ted Tollner, one of my coaches, and Scovil, who eventually turned out to be an okay guy. And like Jim and Linda Kelly, who treated me like a human being right off the bat, when I was nothing. We're still friends, always will be.

Then there were people like Glen Tuckett, the athletic director, a real pain. You remember Nurse Ratched in *One Flew Over the Cuckoo's Nest*? The nurse who was forever leaning on the inmates? That was Glen Tuckett with me. You remember what happened to the nurse, don't you? Jack Nicholson tried to strangle her, choke her, with his own hands.

Admittedly, I wasn't a star student. I was a communications and public relations major, if you can believe that, knowing my regard for the media. One of my classes was newswriting. Your job was to go out and interview people, then come back and write a story. I cut corners, though. I would read the newspaper account of, say, a fire, then rewrite it as though I was there, covering the fire. I'd have been a great sportswriter.

It was a good thing I made it in football, because my success at odd jobs was nil. I had this one task in a dog food factory. My duty there was to take a bag, whip it under this chute where the dog food came out of, get it filled, zip it closed, load it, then run and get another bag—all within about ten seconds. It wasn't long before I was gone. Wanted no part of that.

BYU, always on the lookout for a nice summer job for its

best athletes, found me one pulling weeds for three dollars an hour. That was swell. So was the one shoveling manure at a farm. The guy who owned it asked me to clean out his barn one day. I found a lot of things to clean out, including a dead goat. I was out of there in a hurry, too. I'm not too thrilled about touching goats, even when they're alive.

Without a doubt, though, the highlight of my bizarre BYU experience was meeting this great woman, Nancy Daines. I noticed her in the cafeteria my freshman year. I said to my roommate, Jim Mlott, "She's too nice not to have a boyfriend." But she didn't. And when her roommate asked Jim whether he thought I'd accept Nancy's invitation to go to a dance, I jumped. Hell, yes. We had a great time, and that was the start of a long relationship. February 24, 1978. That was our first date. Whenever February 24 comes around every year, Nancy reminds me. That was our beginning.

In time, the spies around BYU came to think she was a tobacco-chewing alcoholic. She bought a lot of my supplies, and with nothing better to do, some of the folks at BYU would just volunteer to go to supermarkets to keep an eye on things like what students were buying. Sick, but true.

My senior year, Nance and I had a big fight. She was done with beauty school, and wanted to get married, I guess. I wanted some space. I said a bunch of stupid and mean things and told her to go back home to California and forget me. I wanted her to go out with other guys, and yet I didn't. I thought she might go marry someone else, and yet I was hoping she wouldn't. You know how it goes. On the way to the Hula Bowl in Hawaii that year, I stopped by to see her in her home near San Francisco. We'd been in touch since our big fight, but I didn't know whether we'd get back together or not.

Nancy and I had another disagreement while I was at her house. I said, "That's it, I'm going to the car." She followed me out there, and we went for a ride. She started crying. If there's one thing I can't handle—especially from the only woman I ever really loved—it's crying.

"Nancy," I said while we were driving along. "Will you marry me?"

She stopped crying.

I invited her to follow me over to the Hula Bowl. After we returned from Hawaii, I told Nancy's dad about our marriage plans. Her parents were a bit concerned because they knew we'd been having our moments, but they're great people. It's a strong Mormon family; they knew I drank, they saw me drink. But, they accepted me as a human being, the human being who wanted their daughter to be the mother of his children. My parents, of course, were delighted at the news. Then they really went wacko when I didn't ask any of my brothers to be my best man. Homer Jones, a teammate at BYU, a black junior college transfer who helped turn the program around, got the nod. My mother, Roberta, told me she and Dad weren't coming to the wedding.

"Why? What now?" I asked.

"You're having a black best man," said Roberta, another enlightened Mormon.

"Fine," I said. "Don't come."

They came. Nancy and I were married in Utah on May 1, 1982, just after I was drafted by the Bears. The church was nondenominational. I didn't want to get married in a Mormon church, Nance didn't want to get married in a Catholic church, so we split the difference. Everything went well, even though my parents were looking sour. My buddies and I had plenty of beer ordered for the reception, and we used it all.

After we were married, we had our honeymoon in Hawaii, but not before taking a slight detour to Texas for a golf tournament. Nancy understood. She always understands. A great woman, the best thing that ever happened to me. If it wasn't for her, calming me down, I'd probably weigh ninety-five pounds and be hanging out every night at the watering holes on Rush Street in Chicago. I'd probably be living downtown, too. I might be eighty-five pounds.

As for Brigham Young, well, I get the usual alumni letters asking for money. I deposit them in my circular file. I'll give money to a good cause in a minute, but outside Nancy, football, and a few good friends that I met out there, I can't say the college was one of my highlight experiences. Happiness was Provo in the rearview mirror.

Since I left, Brigham Young also has let go of Brent Pratley, my doctor friend. Seems that when my best pal, Pluto, developed that brain tumor a couple of years ago, he called Brent about the problem. Brent looked back in Pluto's medical file at the university and found that there was some information indicating that Pluto could have had a potentially serious illness. But the people in charge of that sort of thing—not Brent—had let it slide.

When Brent relayed that to Pluto, and the authorities and Brigham Young found out, Brent was gone. Remember now, we're talking about an institution that took it upon itself to tell people how to live good lives. I've always suspected that the more those people out there assumed nothing bad was going on, the more bad things were allowed to go on.

Whether it's the media or Brigham Young or anybody else, I'm suspicious when a person or place establishes ground rules for how people should act. I'm talking here about a best friend who could have lost his life. The Mormon spies at BYU? They were worried about whether I was chewing tobacco or having a couple of beers. Nice priorities, huh?

THIRTEEN

My Favorite Sport, Golf

Nancy knows me like a book, of course. And she says I'm not one to come across as too excited around the house, no matter what's happening. Unless it's one of those really nice warm days during the off-season.

"You're playing golf today, aren't you?" she'll say. And, of course, she'll be right.

"The morning before you've got to play a football game," she'll say, "you don't act any different. You're yourself. But, the morning before a game of golf, you're like a little kid. Jumping around like you can't wait."

Well, that's because I can't wait. That's because golf is my favorite sport. I'm not knocking the Bears, I'm not knocking my occupation, I'm not knocking the Super Bowl. I'm not knocking anything. It's just that golf is the best game of all, and by far the most difficult I've ever tried. I watch what those pros do with the ball under pressure, and I'm amazed.

And I do watch golf. I'm not much of one for planning

my schedule around sports events on TV, particularly if the weather is nice. During the football season, I'll usually watch the Monday night game. I'll also watch some baseball, and basketball if I've got nothing else to do. But generally, I'm not much of a spectator.

When there's a golf tournament on, though, if I'm around, I'm usually right in front of the TV set, taking it in from start to finish. Especially if it's one of the major events, like the Masters. Which reminds me of what happened on the first Sunday in April of 1986. It was really warm in Chicago, so I went to play golf with my agent, Steve Zucker, and some friends. We played thirty-six holes, morning and afternoon.

I wasn't in a real good mood when I got back home because I hadn't played real well. Then, I heard that Jack Nicklaus, the greatest golfer ever, shot 30 on the back nine at Augusta National to win the 1986 Masters. I was happy for him, of course, because he's forty-six, and seems like a good guy. I had met him about a month before, at the Nabisco–Dinah Shore LPGA Tournament in Palm Springs, California. He was there for a couple of days because he'd signed with Nabisco to do some work for the company; I was invited to play in the pro-am. I wanted to make sure I shook his hand. Maybe a little of that genius would rub off on me.

Anyway, I got back home that Sunday of the Masters, I heard he won, and I got even madder at myself than I was after playing so rotten. Jack Nicklaus won, and I didn't get to watch it! I should have stayed home. My first thought was, I've got to get a tape of that sucker. I want to see that for myself.

So, you can tell I'm pretty hooked on the game, which may seem strange because here I am earning a living from a violent, sometimes sick sport where people get hurt, where the idea is to hit somebody and hit him hard, where I play a position that makes me the bull's-eye in a target practice. You know, you knock the other team's quarterback out of a game, you've done your duty.

Well, maybe that's what makes golf so special to me; maybe that's why I'll get up at five in the morning to do only two things: go to the bathroom, or play golf. It's you against the ball. You against nature. You against yourself. If football is ninety percent mental at the professional level, then golf has got to be even worse, even more pressure. I don't know how the pros do it, but I admire the hell out of them for it, because I'm not so sure I could. Sometimes, I get a little too wrapped up in how I'm playing.

An example. I was playing in a pro-am not long ago at Rockford, Illinois. One of my partners was Lon Hinkle, a pretty good PGA Tour veteran. I hit a tee shot that I didn't care for, and buried the head of my driver into the tee box. He turned around and just stared at me.

"Son," he said. "You'd never make it on the tour. You just don't have the temperament."

I fear he's right on that count. I'll never suffer a lacerated kidney in golf, but I might just get a hernia. As a release from my anger, I sometimes throw clubs, which is not too smart. I'm not proud of that at all. Nancy said I shouldn't buy any more clubs until I can learn not to throw them. There have been times when I had more clubs spread out on the course than I had in my bag. I'm mellowing, I'm curing it, but I still have my outbursts. A couple of summers ago, I was playing at Kemper Lakes, a terrific course in Hawthorn Woods, Illinois. Kemper Lakes will be host to the 1989 PGA Championship, one of the four major tournaments every year. Kemper Lakes is also properly named. It's got water all over. I hit a shot there and shanked it right into a lake. I was so furious, I threw my 3-wood and shanked it too. Went right into the same pond. "You might want to throw a provisional club," said one of my smart-ass partners, "in case the first one went out-of-bounds."

I started golf relatively late in life. I don't know why I wasn't attracted to it sooner. Maybe because I was so busy with other sports; maybe because I didn't think it was much fun. But, I met a buddy while I was at Brigham Young University—Kevin Tenant, a club pro at the time—and got hooked. He taught me how to play, and even gave me my first set of irons. My insurance man gave me my first set of woods, which is ironic, considering my short fuse.

I've become pretty decent since. A little better each year. My handicap is down to a 10, although I won't argue if you put me down as a 12. I can hit the ball a long way most of the time—300 yards when I've got ahold of it. I really slapped a drive while playing at Pebble Beach after the Super Bowl; it went 347. I enjoyed that. At the prices Pebble Beach charges, you should enjoy your day. My problem, more often than not, is my putting. People say I've got a good stroke, but the day I don't three-putt at least a couple greens is the day I don't play. I don't know what it is. Either I don't concentrate or don't line up putts right. Something. Maybe it has something to do with my bad right eye, the one I stuck a fork into as a child. But I don't want to use my eye as an excuse for why I've got the asbestos hands when it comes to tapping the ball into the hole.

My other big problem is the old scrambled eggs syndrome. I'll be cruising along, playing well, at 2 or 3 over par. Then, I'll do something really dumb, make a grotesque shot, and take a 7 or an 8. That does it. I'm cooked. I keep thinking about what Corey Pavin, that hotshot young pro, said about his game, that the key for him was learning to hold his temper. But, I'll take an 8, and take a powder. Ruins my round. My mind becomes scrambled eggs. It's a lot different from football in that respect. In football, you tend to play better when you're mad. Not so in golf. At least, not for me.

I have had some memorable rounds, though. My best score was at a course in Utah, Springville, which isn't long but has plenty of trees and water. I also shot a 75 at Medinah No. 3, probably the toughest course in the Chicago area and one of the best in the world. The U.S. Open is going there in 1990. I think I hit only two fairways that day, and was constantly swinging out of the trees, which are all over that place. But I was unconscious. I'd get into trouble off the tee, and wind up on the green.

I'm not much of a safety-first golfer, and that attitude helped me that day. I attack the ball and take my chances, even if I tee off with a 1-iron instead of a wood—which I do often, to keep it straight. I believe you have to play aggressively, which is why I wonder why Curtis Strange took so much heat for the way he played the last few holes of the 1985 Masters. He was leading the tournament, then got into trouble by shooting for the green and winding up in the water. Then he was criticized for being too much of a gambler.

Heck, on one of the shots that went splash, he only had about 200 yards to the pin. It wasn't that he made a bad decision, it was that he made a bad swing. Even though Augusta National can be a bear, I don't think you win there or anyplace else by laying up. You don't earn a half-million dollars, like he did in 1985, by being conservative, either. If it was me in that situation, I'd have done the same thing. Let it fly. Here I am talking like that, and I go wacko when I lose two dollars on a round to somebody like Jay Hilgenberg, who I give four shots a side and then he plays the round of his life.

Except for my 3-putts and 4-putts, I really enjoy a day of golf. Not only the challenge, but the idea of getting out in the fresh air, out in nature, without any telephones. It's a complete release from tensions and aggravations . . . at least until you get angry over doing something stupid. I also enjoy the many tournaments I play in where us so-called celebrities are teamed with businessmen. Most of these events are for good charitable causes, and most of them are good times. I meet and talk with people I'd otherwise never get a chance to know, and probably never try to get to know. You never know when you're going to make a connection. You never know when you're going to need a parking ticket fixed.

Shooting the breeze about golf is our common denominator. I'd rather talk about golf than football any day, especially with a legend like Bob Hope. I did a TV special with him one night in New Orleans before the Super Bowl, and we wound up talking for a long time about our golf games. Not football, not television. Golf. It was great. Hilgenberg liked the idea so much when I told him about it that he went back up to Hope's hotel suite at two o'clock in the morning to wake him up. But that's another story. Jay didn't so much want to talk golf as he wanted another crack at the sandwich tray. I stuck my foot in my mouth earlier in the evening when Bob and I were gabbing on about how much we loved the sport.

"Yeah," he said, "it sure is a great game."

"Yeah," I said, "you can keep playing until you're eighty."

I didn't find out until later that Bob Hope is over eighty. I thought he was about sixty or sixty-five.

Oh, well. We still hit it off. When his people asked me if they could do anything for me in exchange for taking the time out to tape the show, I had the answer all ready.

"Yeah," I said. "I'd like to play in Bob's tournament."

A few weeks later, I got a note from Hope inviting me to his annual event in Palm Springs, the Bob Hope–Chrysler Classic. Five days in heaven during the brutally cold month of January. Obviously, because it falls the week after the NFL Conference Championship, I won't be playing in it next year if we make it to the Super Bowl again. Unless coach Mike Ditka, another golfaholic, gives me five days off from practice, which I'm not planning on.

But, hopefully, I'll be out there one of these days. I have this fantasy about winning the Masters, or coming back after my football career to join the Seniors' Tour. Remember, I said fantasy. For now, my off-season enjoyment is running off to as many tournaments as I can fit in. Like in Texas every June for a children's cancer treatment center in El Paso. Terry Bradshaw used to do it when he still was quarterbacking for the Pittsburgh Steelers, and invited me every year. When he couldn't keep doing it, I wound up lending my name to the tournament. In honor of me, they might want to have a logo with a broken club on it.

There are also a lot of those one-day pro-am events around Chicago, a great golfing area with some sensational courses. The Bears are involved in one, the Brian Piccolo Tournament, named after the team's former running back who died of cancer in the prime of his life. The greatest restaurant in the world—Gus Cappas's The Prime Minister, minutes from my home—even has a shotgun affair every June, which I make every effort to attend, even if the course isn't the greatest. It's like trying to play in the middle of a driving range. Tees close to greens, balls flying everywhere. Wearing helmets is advised. That doesn't bother me, though. I'll play golf in the rain, in the wind, in the snow, if I have to. I'd like to get really good at this crazy game.

"You're going to pull up in a Winnebago one day," Nancy says. "You're going to pack your golf clubs and just disappear for about a month. Aren't you? You'll play in all fifty states, then come back home." (She forgot Canada. Nice courses up there, too.)

And then, when I retire, maybe I can fulfill another dream. You know how *Golf Digest* magazine lists the top hundred golf courses every year? I'd like to just get on a plane and play them, one after another. What a way to live.

If I played golf that much, I might even get over my case of the jitters whenever I step up to the first tee in one of those charity deals. There always seems to be a gallery around to check out the athletes or movie stars in the celebrity category, and damned if I don't worry about whiffing and making a fool out of myself. I don't approach a football game with nerves like that. I don't worry about throwing interceptions in a Super Bowl that a hundred million people are watching, but I worry about missing the ball in front of fifty people. You figure it out. It must be that I'm a lot more comfortable at football than golf. I've played football longer and better, I guess. I also get more easily bored at football than golf. But, I know that I can handle getting tackled by a bunch of animals who want to see me leave the field on a stretcher; I'm not so sure I can handle many more 3-putts, though, before I turn myself into a basket case.

Are golfers athletes? You hear that question a lot, and my answer would be absolutely yes. I'm not sure, judging by a look at some of those bodies out on the pro tour, that all of them can run a mile. But they don't have to, so why do it? As a professional athlete, you do what you have to do to stay on top of your game, and that doesn't always mean pumping iron or jogging every morning. There are a lot of athletes in other sports whose physiques don't belong in bathing suits, but they succeed. You can be a star in sports without being a star at the beach. Noah Jackson, who used to play for the Bears, wasn't exactly a Greek god, but could he hit a golf ball. Then there's Jim Thorpe, an excellent pro golfer who used to play some football. He still looks like he could break somebody in half.

Golfers have to prepare for a different kind of existence, anyway. They have to stay in control; they can't take their frustrations out like most other athletes; they lead very lonely lives out there. If sports is supposed to be a mixture of mental and physical toughness, I don't know how you can get much tougher mentally than golf.

I wish I had more discipline at golf, particularly in the area of practicing. Every once in a while, I'll go up to Kemper Lakes, where the former hockey star Stan Mikita is the pro. (That might be a nice thing for me to think about after football . . . a club pro somewhere.) He'll take a look at me and offer a few suggestions, but usually, I like to just show up and play. I'm not much of one for practicing and hitting balls, which is bad, but I'm sure a lot of other people are that way, too. All the more reason to admire the pros and all the time they spend on the practice tee, just slashing balls by themselves until their hands bleed.

It's a strange game, golf. I feel excited for the team when the Bears win, but when I win a match or play well, I feel good for myself, a completely different emotion. Likewise, if you screw up in football, you feel like you let the team down. But, probably someone will come over and console you. In golf, if you botch a shot, you've got only yourself to curse, and nobody will come over and say, "We'll get 'em next series."

Bobby Clampett, one of the touring pros now, went to Brigham Young. We didn't run in the same circles, and besides, he didn't attend there on the five-year plan like I did. We never really got to know each other, but he did one thing I envy, talking about fantasies. He played three rounds of golf in one day over what must have been six thousand miles. He woke up in Scotland, played there, jumped a jet for New York, where he played eighteen holes at Winged Foot, then hopped a plane for California, where he played eighteen at Pebble Beach before nightfall.

I have met and admired some other pros, like Nicklaus, Lee Trevino, Ray Floyd, plus several of the women pros, who I saw at the Nabisco Tournament. Also Johnny Miller, Lanny Wadkins, and Fuzzy Zoeller. You have to like Fuzzy's attitude. I met Sam Snead, an interesting old guy. I also ran into my newest hero, Payne Stewart, at Grand Cypress outside Orlando. He was just hitting practice shots one day, when he came over and gave me a few tips—one of which I'm using now, and it's helping. A knock-down eight-iron punch shot out of trouble. Feet close together, ball back in your stance, finish with a low follow-through. Thank you, Payne Stewart.

My other hero has to be Craig Stadler. Not only is he a good player, but he's got a bit of a short fuse like me. I remember what he did at the U.S. Open at Winged Foot in 1984. He was having a terrible day, when he stepped up to a tee shot and whiffed. Stone-cold whiffed it! Then he got mad at himself, giving himself the choke sign. Then he kicked the ball off the tee, and walked off the course. Withdrew! That's the way to go, Craig. You can't let this game get you down. When it's not your day, it's not your day.

My golfing etiquette closely resembles that at times, which is why I don't know whether I'll ever be the country-club type. First of all, my idea of a nice afternoon is playing with no shirt and no shoes or socks. That won't work at fancy places, but I wonder whether most people realize how nice it is to walk through the grass in bare feet. Particularly on the greens. It's a great sensation, getting right down to nature. It's like an expensive carpet, only better.

The dress code at most of those plush clubs is a little annoying to me. Part of the enjoyment of playing golf on a beautiful day is getting some sun, but when they say you can wear shorts, they mean shorts that practically come down to your knees. You might as well wear knickers, like my pal Payne. I'd rather wear shorter shorts, shorts that probably show a little too much thigh. But, at least you keep your tan.

My wife, who buys practically all my clothes, has done some heavy shopping for me in the last couple of years. Now I not only have some nice golf clothes, I have some nice golf clothes that actually match. I even look like a golfer now. Some people probably are leery of inviting me to a nice club or a nice tournament, because they're afraid I'm going to show up all unruly, wearing just a headband, drinking beer, and acting crazy. Well, I respect the sport too much for that, and besides, I like the social element of playing different places and meeting different people.

On the other hand, Zucker has this theory about me.

"Jim," he says, "if you had one wish, it would be to buy your own golf course, and play naked."

I can't argue with that, although I'd never have a total tan because I need a glove. It would be nice, though, to have your own place to yourself. Hire a great designer, like Jack Nicklaus, to build it just the way you want . . . tough, with lots of sand and water, but not so bad that the average person can't play it. Then, you could invite whoever you wanted out, whenever. I'd have refreshment stands every few holes. I'd have no carts, because half the fun of golf is walking. Carts ruin the game. I'd also do my best to have lights put in, so I could play some night golf, too. People like to play cards and things after playing golf. Not me. I like to play golf until the sun goes down. With lights, I'd be in heaven. Either that, or maybe I can invent some kind of ball that will glow in the dark. I could throw a club and not disturb anybody. Beautiful. But expensive.

Until then, I'll play wherever I can whenever I can. Even if I keep 3-putting. It's better to play a bad round of golf than not to play at all.

FOURTEEN

Who I Am, and Why

Shortly after Super Bowl XX, I went to Los Angeles to make a couple of stops, one of which was Johnny Carson's *Tonight Show*. I bumped into Buddy Hackett, the comedian, backstage.

"Don't ever change," he said. "Don't try to please everybody, because it'll never work."

Interesting, because earlier that day, I was receiving an award at Hugh Hefner's Playboy Mansion when someone came in, huffing and puffing, asking me for a comment on a blast leveled at me by Joe Theismann, the Washington Redskins' quarterback. He was at a speaking engagement in Canada, where he ripped me for being a bad "role model." He said that if the youth of America followed my example, they'd all grow up to be beer-drinking yo-yos, or something like that. "I don't respond to someone who can't punt a football more than one yard," I replied, referring to Theismann's hilarious shank job against the Bears in our fourth game of the regular season.

I was pretty proud of that comeback, which just sort of rolled off my tongue. Some friends of mine said it was a devastating put-down, and, whatever prompted Theismann to think twice, he did. He apologized the next day.

But Hackett was right on. He doesn't have to apologize for the way he thinks, and I don't believe I have to, either. I'm a little skeptical about this business of role models. I mean, Theismann left his wife and children. Theismann is full of himself, always kissing behinds and self-promoting. I respect him as a quarterback, but is he a good role model, whatever that term means? Does he think youngsters should grow up like that?

If I'm supposed to be a role model because I'm a high-profile athlete—you know, quarterback of a Super Bowl team—then the best thing I can advise is, be yourself. Don't operate to please other people; don't mold yourself to satisfy society. Be yourself. That doesn't mean you don't have to obey certain obvious rules; that doesn't mean you can't love, can't share, can't be a decent human being.

But once you wake up in the morning worrying about what other people are going to think, and once you go to bed worrying about what other people are going to think, you'll lose the ability to think for yourself, to be yourself. You'll lose all individuality, and the very thing you might be seeking—popularity, approval, whatever—you won't get anyway. Like Hackett said, you're never going to please everybody, so what's the sense in trying?

I was once told—by a sportswriter in Utah, if you can believe it—that I was the most mentally tough person he'd ever met. I appreciated that. I took it as one of the ultimate compliments, because being mentally tough is the best way to see through all the restrictions society establishes for no reason, other than the fact that too much of society is afraid to let go, to go with the flow, to enjoy.

I've been a bit tough on my parents, and a bit tough on

Brigham Young. But I'm glad I went through childhood the way I did, glad I went through college the way I did. It helped me become independent and forced me to make a lot of decisions on my own. I don't think it's so much that I grew up a rebel; it's that I grew up faster than most kids. That isn't all bad. In fact, that's the only way to be. I've endured more pain and pressure than ninety percent of the people who are trying to tell me how to live. I don't depend on anyone; I don't rely on anyone. Maybe that's the underdog in me. I pull for underdogs; I often feel like one myself.

You can't keep telling kids, "You can't do this . . . you can't do that." That's why so many children are sheltered, why they can't cope with really important things when it comes time. Children are naturally adventurous. Children want to explore things. If you take all the mystery out of life, if you make a child into a robot, I think you hurt not only a youngster's sense of adventure, but his sense of achievement. For all the hell I caused, for all the hell I put up with, I knew where I was headed, what I wanted to do—play sports. You think if I wasn't achievement-oriented, I would have played with all these broken bones over the years?

Trial and error. That's the best way. I'll give you an example. I smoked my first marijuana joint when I was fourteen years old. But I realized it's not good for you, and I stopped. I didn't have to see any guidance counselor, or attend any rehabilitation center. I just decided on my own. I can't be sure, but I'm guessing if I had been pampered, if I'd grown up having everything I wanted when I wanted it, maybe I wouldn't have been strong enough to realize something like that on my own. Maybe if I hadn't had broomsticks broken over my back, or hadn't been whipped with belts, I'd have grown up a mental wimp.

I'm not saying I'd ever do that to my children. Ashley and Sean I can't hug enough. I can't love them enough, can't give them enough attention. But when it comes time for them to start getting a feel of what life's all about, I'm not going to put them in a cage, I'm not going to isolate them. I'm going to let them absorb a few knocks, let them figure out on their own what they like and don't like. And, hopefully, if they want to talk to me, they'll be relaxed enough to treat me not only as a father, an authority figure, but as their best friend.

If I don't feel that way about my parents now, well, that's just the way it is. It's probably too late to fix. But I came out of it alright, and I've got to take into consideration their upbringing, too. When I was a kid, I heard all the stories about how my mom and dad had to walk five miles to school, all uphill, and all that. Maybe they weren't ready to deal with my attitude toward all their rules; maybe it was partly their rules that account for my attitude. I don't know. It doesn't matter, because I survived. A couple of my school buddies are dead. Maybe if things had been different, I'd have wound up like them. My parents did me a favor in the end. I didn't end up a spoiled brat. A little bit of a brat, maybe. But not spoiled. And for all I've done, I've never been arrested, or, for that matter, killed. Two miracles there.

Not that I'm proud of some of the stunts I've pulled off along the way. I probably didn't have to take off all my clothes when I went to that dance at Weber State years ago, but I did. I probably didn't have to come home drunk at three-thirty in the morning a couple of St. Patrick's Days ago, and fall in the driveway face first so hard that I broke my glasses, and wind up having to peel my bloody face off the pillow at six the next night with Nancy giving me the evil eye. But I did. And one other thing. When I did those things, and a hundred other weird things, I didn't hurt anybody. I did them to myself, nobody else.

That's the way it is now, but to read some of the accounts of my alleged escapades, you'd think I was one of the Hell's Angels, roaming the countryside at night, raping and pillaging and burning. Some of the people who think I'm the devil on earth should see me at home most nights, playing with the kids, changing Sean's diapers. But they won't see me, because I don't want them to. Why? It goes back to what I said earlier. I don't care what they think, because it doesn't matter.

I will admit I wasn't always such a "humanitarian" when it came to not hurting others. There was this crippled girl at elementary school in San Jose. She wore braces because of polio. I'd make a point of locking the gate at the school every once in a while. It was only about a six-foot gate, but it was like a mountain to her. She'd have to try to climb the thing, and she'd usually wind up all tangled, hanging upside down. All because of me. Why did I do that? Who knows? You're young and inconsiderate. Why did I stick tacks in that fat Hawaiian kid's butt? We all do things like that.

But now, when I see a kid on crutches or in a wheelchair, it makes me sick. I might run by a thousand groupies wanting autographs after a game, but if I see a kid who's hurting, I'll stop and go back. I think of how happy I was when Ashley and Sean were born with all their arms, all their legs. I have lots of time for children. It's the adults in the world that create most of the problems for kids to solve.

For all my mental toughness, I admit I can still be somewhat gullible, especially when it comes to money. After Jerry Argovitz stopped handling my financial affairs, and before Steve Zucker, my current representative, took over, there was a guy in between. I met him around Chicago playing golf, which should have told me right away that he didn't have all his marbles. He talked big, like he knew how to invest for me and all that. Then he asked me if I'd let him do my money matters for a year. If I didn't like how he operated after then, fine. I could move on to somebody else.

I figured there would be no problem in that. Here was a local guy who seemed fair enough. Only when I checked into my bank account a few months later did I realize that the guy was robbing me blind. He wound up with authorization to cash checks from good old trusting me. I thought I could lay my hands on about $40,000 to buy Nancy a car. I wound up with only about $10,000 in there. This guy had put the rest in his pocket. Zucker, who had warned me about him, went after him. We were going to sue, but the night before we were headed for court, this guy suddenly came up with the money he owed me. Later on, I ran into somebody he'd stolen from to pay me.

I don't know how people like that can sleep at night. We had another incident during the 1985 football season with this recording, the "Super Bowl Shuffle." A friend of Willie Gault's came up with this brainstorm about having the Bears do this song, and then the proceeds would go to charity, to help feed needy families at Christmastime.

I didn't care for the idea of singing about how great we were with half the season to go. It was just the kind of thing that could boomerang on the Bears, and get everybody mad at us. I did want to help the hungry, though, and Willie and his pal kept giving us the line about how they needed Walter Payton and me to participate to give it credibility, to help it sell.

Well, I went and did the audio version, but then they released the thing a lot earlier than I thought they would. Right in the middle of our schedule. That got me angry, and when they wanted me to do the video version, I refused. I missed the taping session and so did Wally. Zucker got worried, after a few calls from the organizer, that we'd be sued. So I eventually went through with it and so did Wally. You can see, if you look closely, how they sort of patched us in to appear as though we were with the rest of the players, who did it together, before us.

The end of this story is that we found out that only about fifty percent of the money went to feed the needy. I don't know how much went to Willie's friend, who it turned out was in debt because of some other venture. I don't know exactly where Willie figured in, and I don't want to know. I do want to know how people get away with certain things in broad daylight. I don't understand that any more than I understand why the farmers in this country are getting screwed while there are so many people going hungry.

That's one area where I don't have to worry. My conscience. I will kick myself on occasion for not signing an autograph, or for saying something really outrageous. But basically, I can rest easy with what I do because I don't cheat anybody, and I don't lie to anybody. I don't have to worry today about what I told somebody yesterday and whether it'll be the same as what I tell that person tomorrow. I don't want anybody to cater to me.

I do a lot of things on impulse, things that I take as harmless. For instance, I occasionally wear this T-shirt. On the front, it says, "Adolf Hitler's European Tour, 1939–45." On the back of it is a list of the places he tried to overcome, or tried to and failed. Like, "September 1939—Poland." Then, "September 1940—England, canceled," with a big line drawn through it. One of the Chicago reporters, always anxious to portray me as evil, wrote about the shirt, and Zucker, who's Jewish, needled me, too. I was with him when I bought the thing in Myrtle Beach for twenty dollars. We both laughed.

But some people didn't see any laughs in it, so I got more bad publicity. Probably some of the people who hated me for it are the same ones who go to the office every day and do everything they can to finish a big business deal, including cut somebody else's heart out. If I do any harm by wearing a shirt like that, it's unintentional. It's an innocent action, if a little weird. But when people hurt other people on purpose, that's different.

And it all goes back to what I believe as a way of life. Do your thing, and let others sweat about what's supposed to be right and wrong. I have no time for that sort of thing. I spend my energy on worrying about my friends and family; I don't have any time or energy to worry about my enemies, my critics. I will not be a puppet, I will not be swayed by others' ideals or what they think I should be or what they want me to be.

I don't like phonies or people who are afraid of their shadows. Likewise, I don't especially enjoy people who don't have a sense of humor. If you want to be my friend—and *I'll* make that decision—you've got a better chance if you can make me laugh. We tend to take things much too seriously, particularly ourselves. There's nobody who makes more fun of Jim McMahon than Jim McMahon, but damned if people didn't get all bent out of shape when I came up with that ridiculous haircut in training camp a year ago. They were knocking me for what I did to my head. It was nobody else's head. It was *my* head. And I just did it for something to do. But people got all worked up. I'm not so sure I'm not more sane than the ninety percent of the people in this world who think I'm nuts.

These are the same levelheaded folks, remember, who run up to you in the street squealing for a silly signature on a silly piece of paper. It always starts out pretty much the same way, usually, "I hate to bother you, but . . ." And then they might follow up with something really inane like, "Do you really know Walter Payton?" Or, "Do you really know The Refrigerator?" Not only do I know them, I shower with them every day.

That's part of the reason why I'd just as soon "hermitize" myself most of the time. At Brigham Young, most of the people knew the Jim McMahon who threw the football on Saturdays. They didn't know anything about the Jim McMahon otherwise. That would be fine in Chicago, too, if I could just play the games on Sundays and vanish the rest of the week, or get away with a disguise.

I do like to go out and have a few beverages with the guys, like we do on Thursday nights during the season. But, while I enjoy that, I enjoy staying at home with Nancy and the kids just as much, or more. When I go to dinner, or fly someplace for an appearance, I'll usually take Nance along, because I want her along. But we're perfectly content to stay home, eat dinner, and just relax. We'll seldom set a table or do anything fancy. She's a great cook, and very understanding, too. If I'm watching something I like on TV, she'll bring my plate right to the recliner, and we'll all eat there. Then, later on, she might make some popcorn, and I'll have a beverage or two, and I'm in heaven. I don't have to be in public, getting the star treatment I don't care for anyway. I'd just as soon be at home, where I'm only No. 4 in the household. Behind the kids and Nancy, which is perfect.

We have met some great people in Chicago, a few outside football, and it's a great night when we can just have a few couples over to unwind. The natural tendency is to hang out with fellow football players and their wives or girlfriends. We're a pretty close bunch on the Bears; we're basically in the same age range. Plus—and this goes back to having some laughs—athletes by nature have a certain sense of humor. At least *I've* found that. We play a game for a living, usually a pretty good living. It's not a life-and-death situation, and that lends itself to jokes, pranks, and so forth. Right up my alley.

Earlier on, I brought up some words to describe our team. If you asked me to do the same for myself, I'd probably do something like this: shy, generous, impulsive, tough, easygoing, thirsty, competitive, dependable, solid, basic, compassionate. I realize some of those words seem contradictory, but so am I, I guess. So are we all, from day to day. I do feel I'm all of those things at one time or another.

The more hours I spend around glad-handers and acquaintances who think they're your friends, the more I'd like to melt into the background. I see the double standards, how Nance will go into a store where the clerk won't give her the time of day. Then, the next time, I might go in with her, and the clerk will recognize me, and it's a different story. If that doesn't make you leery of people, nothing will.

I might seem as though I enjoy all the commotion surrounding a football player, but I really don't. I feel uncomfortable when somebody buys me dinner or a drink. Buy it for somebody who can't afford it. That's where I turn in, and almost become bashful. Those are the times when I wish I was back home in my recliner, surrounded by just the kids and Nancy.

Another surprise, readers. For all the way I've been portrayed, I do believe in God, in a supreme being. I wouldn't call myself religious, but you look around and see your children growing up, and you know this world isn't just an accident. It didn't just happen. I thank the Man Upstairs for giving the gifts I've got. I thank Him for more than you think. I'm not sure why I'm so lucky; maybe I'll pay in my next life. I even was Jesus once in a school play, robe and all. I don't want to find out about the other place, so I hope I do enough good things to wind up in heaven, even if they do have to relax the entrance requirements.

I don't think you have to be a model citizen twenty-four hours a day—there I go again with people imposing values on other people. But, there's a place for giving, and there are people who need it. I mentioned that golf tournament I help with every June in Texas. Normally, I guess, celebrities get paid to attend. From the first year I went there, I've always written out a check when I leave. They kind of freak out down there. They can't believe it. But what's the big deal? I can afford it. Why not?

Before you get the idea that I'm perfect, whoa. I'm not even close. I swear too much, and I'm not happy about it. That's a habit I'd like to cut out, especially now that the kids are starting to understand and repeat. If I can't cure myself, pretty soon Nance and I will have to cure them.

I chew tobacco, too, which is another vice I'd like to bag. I've heard all the stories about cancer, and I'm not anxious to find out firsthand, or first-lip. I've cut out chewing on occasion, for long periods, and I'd like to keep trying until I succeed for good.

I don't let myself cry, no matter what the situation, and that's probably nothing more than the machismo in me taking over. I guess if I cry, I feel I'm showing too much of me, letting too much of me out. And I like to keep most of what's inside me right where it belongs. Inside. I can love and hug and kiss and never say no to a friend. But I wouldn't call myself the romantic type. I don't get all excited on Valentine's Day, which means I'll probably forget to send Nance a card.

I'm cocky, yes, and a little bit of a hot dog. But again, I don't think these are necessarily bad traits. The guys who see me day in and day out, my teammates, know my cockiness in a different way. They know I can't stand to lose, that I can't stand to lose because I'm not accustomed to it, and that I don't plan to lose. I don't think I'm abrasive in that respect. Because I think I'm a winner, too. There. That's another adjective. I've won wherever I've gone.

I've also ruffled some feathers by having a little hot dog in me, but again, I don't see that I'm doing any great damage. We are entertainers in an entertainment business. Show a little flair. Have a little fun. Have a little fun with yourself. I make myself laugh. I think I can make other people laugh, but if people don't know how to take me, that's fine. I don't want them to be my friends anyway, so why not keep them guessing? Why not play with their minds? They play with my reputation, right? It would be a lot easier for me if I were on better terms with more people, but so what? I play a little dumber than I really am. Most people are going to believe the worst about you, and the people I don't care about, I'm not going to worry about correcting. Too many people conform because they're afraid not to. There are a lot of people who would like to do what I do, act a little loose once in a while, but they're afraid. Then I read newspaper stories, or letters from parents, full of hate for me and what I represent to them. Absolute freedom. I wonder if sometimes people who jump all over me aren't a little jealous. Not because I'm a football player with a lot of money. Because I have the conviction to be free.

If people get all upset because I wear an Adidas logo, then that's their problem. If they get all upset because they think I'm out drinking beer every night when I'm home eating popcorn, that's their problem. I know this. If I drank as much as I've read that I drink, I wouldn't still be alive to read about it. I like my beverages, like them a lot. I don't show up to Soldier Field every Sunday hammered, though. Sorry to disappoint.

But, let 'em have their fun, these people imagining what I'm really like. They'll never know, because I'll never let them know. I'll do my shot in public, whether it's playing football or whatever, and then I'll come home, where only my friends and family come through the door. Only they will know what I'm all about. My values, I don't wear them on my uniform.

I can tell you, though, that I don't want to be a nice guy as much as I want to be a good guy. And, remember, if I shave my head, it's my head. I'm not hurting your head, or anybody else's head. It's my business. And what's going on inside my head is my business, too. Unless you're a friend.

FIFTEEN

What Next?

Last May 1 was our fourth wedding anniversary.

"Happy anniversary," I said to Nance.

"You remembered," she said, laughing.

"Let's go to lunch, just you and me," I said. We jumped in the car and headed out. "Where are we going, Jim?" she asked after a few minutes.

"We're going for a ride," I said.

"A ride?" she said. "Since when do we just get in a car and leave the kids behind with a baby-sitter for the afternoon, just to take a ride?"

I didn't say much. I didn't have to when we drove up to a beautiful three-plus-acre lot, just a few miles from where we rent a town house now in Northbrook. There was a sign in front of the vacant lot, and I pulled the car up so Nancy could read it:

"Sold to Jim and Nancy McMahon."

She started crying. (God, I hate crying.)

"Happy anniversary," I said again.

That's where our dream home will be, someday soon. Nance had been looking around, and fell in love with the plot of land. I didn't say much when I first saw it, and she probably didn't think I'd go for the almost $500,000 tab, which would buy a lot of Mooseheads. But I got to work on it, and had the real estate people post that sign just for those few minutes when we drove up on our anniversary. If Nance wants it, it's hers.

Besides, we'd been talking for some time about settling in Chicago instead of California, where I once figured I'd wind up establishing roots. If you can handle the winters around Chicago, it's a great city. Fortunately for my health, I'm married, so I can leave Rush Street to the young and frisky. If I were single in Chicago, I might not see thirty.

"Jim," Steve Zucker told me when we were still debating about where to live the rest of our lives, "if you stayed around Chicago, you could own this city."

Well, I don't really want to own Chicago. I just want to own a home that will give Nance whatever she desires, and give me as much privacy as possible. I think our dream home will do the trick.

She wants a big kitchen, three big bedrooms, a playroom for the kids, a family room, and all that. I'd like a racquetball court downstairs, so I don't have to go to the Bears' headquarters in Lake Forest to play. I'd also like a small weight and exercise room downstairs for when I want to keep this finely tuned body of mine in shape. A swimming pool, a Jacuzzi, fireplaces all over. No matter how much I'd want one, I don't think a portable pottie near my recliner would work, although it would be nice not to have to get up even to relieve myself. I'll settle for a remote-control TV flicker; maybe even a remote-control beer tap.

"You can't just sit there and watch TV all day after you retire," Nance once scolded me. Then she paused for about a minute. "On second thought," she said, "maybe you can."

She knows me. I might be a little crazy, but I'm a lot lazy. If things go well, I'd like to even build a Taco Bell and a Wendy's out front, so I won't have to go far for a lunch. Maybe a 31 Flavors, too, for the kids. That way, I'd only really have to leave home for games, practice, golf, and a few appearances. The rest of the time, we could "hermitize," with just friends coming over. No strangers welcome.

I'm not very fancy. I don't like sit-down dinners, and the first time I saw a fingerbowl, I didn't know whether to drink it or plant something in it. Jewelry isn't for me, either. I wear a chain and a watch and no rings. The wedding ring is put away somewhere for safekeeping. I doubt if I'll wear my Super Bowl ring. First, I'll have it appraised, to see if the Bears' management really spent some money on it.

I would like a few frills around the home, though. I saw this mansion out in Pebble Beach, California, with a tee area in the backyard, complete with ball washer, plus three putting greens—one 50 yards away, another at 100, another at 150. That would be sensational, but if we also want a small lake for water skiing, I might have to settle for just a putting green in the back. Lord knows, the way I putt, I could use the practice.

And that's where I'll be until I become senile. Don't call me. I'll call you. By that time in my life, maybe my image will change with the public, and maybe even the press. I'm not expecting that, or losing any sleep worrying about that, but anything's possible. If I wind up not being thought of as a jerk by so many people, that would be nice, but not necessary. For that to happen, other people will have to change, not me. I'm going to continue doing things my way. If I go into a bar for a few beverages, I'll hope to slide in the back door, unnoticed. Same if I go to a hospital to visit a sick child.

I do remember meeting Joe Namath early last season, when he came to Chicago to interview me for ABC. I never had many idols. I never was much of a hero-worshiper, or jock-sniffer, or autograph-seeker. I liked Mickey Mantle, I think Jack Nicholson is super, and I always admired Joe Willie Namath, which made our little visit special. If there's one person who I identify with in sports, it's Namath.

If I recall correctly, Joe Willie had to put up with his share of grief when he came to the New York Jets, a highly paid hotshot quarterback from Alabama. He was very controversial, dressed real flashy, and talked flamboyantly. He had the courage to predict the Jets would pull a huge upset over the Baltimore Colts in Super Bowl III, 1969, and the American Football League was considered a weak sister, a cheap imitation of the NFL. They all laughed at Joe Willie. More than laugh, they ripped him.

But Namath not only had the conviction to say what he felt, he also had the ability to back it up. The Jets won, just like he said they would. As his career went on, he sort of grew on people. He went from being looked at as some kind of a wacko to a damn good guy. When he was introduced to the crowd before Super Bowl XX in New Orleans, he got a tremendous ovation.

Well, maybe if I'm introduced at a Super Bowl in twenty years, I'll get some applause, too. Maybe the media won't be ragging me so much by then. Maybe. I'm not going to give in to them. I'm not going to work on it.

What I have to work on, besides my atrocious putting, is keeping the Bears as champions. There could be only one thing sweeter than winning the Super Bowl once. That's winning it twice, and then three times, and then four times. As I've said before, I think we have what it takes. We have a lot of players who are famous; we also have a lot of players like a Mark Bortz, ornery and gifted, but a guy who doesn't get much publicity. It's a good nucleus, a young nucleus. Will management work to keep that nucleus? Will management try to compensate for the players like Al Harris and Todd Bell, who we've apparently lost forever because of contract hassles? Will management attempt to find some quality replacements for Leslie Frazier and Dennis McKinnon, outstanding players we've lost for just a while, hopefully, because of injuries? Well, those are key questions concerning our immediate future.

We've been there once. We know how good we are, how hungry we are. We feel as though we're the only ones who can keep ourselves from becoming better and better. We had some great players playing last year with a lot of hurts. Guys like Dan Hampton and Steve McMichael. Totally unselfish with their bodies. You know that solid people like that won't let down. You know that as long as Mike Singletary can walk, he's not going to let complacency creep in.

They say that repeating as champions is difficult, and it is. But I, for one, won't ever let the offense feel comfortable just because we've got one Super Bowl ring. And, knowing the guys on defense like I do, the kind of pride and desire they have, I can't see them not doing their damnedest to keep this thing going. It's too good, too rare, an opportunity to let slip by. We don't want to finish our careers kicking ourselves. We want to finish kicking our opponents, burying them.

There's no doubt that, because we were the way we were during our Super Bowl year, other teams will be laying for us. They have to resent not only the fact that we dominated the league by being so good yet so clean; they have to also resent the fact that we made a point of having such a ball playing football. We didn't poke fun at other teams by saying inflammatory things about them; we just had fun, among ourselves, by doing and saying outrageous things, period. We not only knew how to play, we knew how to party. That had to infuriate opponents almost as much as getting beaten by us 44–0. By the time you read this, we'll already have played our 1986 exhibition season opener in London, England, against the Dallas Cowboys. As soon as I saw that baby pop up on the schedule, I thought to myself, After what we did to them last year, those goody-goody Cowboys will be treating that game in August like it's the Super Bowl.

Check it out to see if I was wrong.

More than anything, that kind of swagger we have can come back and haunt you, unless you're ready and willing to pay the price again. I think we are; I'm confident we will be. The fork in the road might be the players' attitude toward management. If we keep getting the hint that our owner isn't as committed as we are, that could also be trouble. Then, you might have players all over, not just on the Bears, asking themselves the same question: Is it worth it? Is it worth it to bust our tails? Then, you've got an attitude problem that goes beyond winning and losing. Then you rob players of their spirit, our greatest asset besides physical talent. I worry about something like that. I worry a lot.

I don't exactly know what happened to the 1963 world champion Bears. I was still too young. I was just a mere gleam in my father's broomstick then. But I've talked to some players from that team, like Ed O'Bradovich and Davey Whitsell. I've heard there were no bonuses or anything like that from George Halas for a job well done. The players went all the way, and got just the NFL winner's share. Halas gave a lot of money to charities, but apparently he didn't believe in that old saying about how charity begins at home. The next year, same basic team, the Bears were 5–9. That's what I mean about losing your spirit. I hope it never happens with us, although I'm afraid it could. I hope we have another great season. I hope we have a lot of great seasons before I'm done with the Bears. I hope we don't outgrow management to the point where we go backward. And I hope we get off to another good start, because I know what will happen: "Boooo!!"

Yep, our wonderful fans will be all over us again. They said our fans were unbelievably loud during the playoff games in Chicago against the Giants and Rams last January. I agree.

I also ask, Why shouldn't they have been? Any city's fans will get behind a winner; it's the fans who stick by you when things aren't going well that you appreciate more.

In my own style of making friends, I was one of the first Bear players to wonder why so many fans at our home games the last couple of years seemed to arrive with laryngitis. They sat on their hands. It was like a graveyard at times. Chicago fans are great? What about the people in places like Seattle, where the noise level is so loud you can't hear yourself think? They've never won a Super Bowl in that town, but you wouldn't know it.

It wasn't too long ago, don't forget, that the city of Chicago would have to wait until the last minute to find out if the blackout would be lifted for Bear home games. That's the NFL rule stating that, unless all the tickets are sold seventy-two hours in advance, there's no television. We had a few of those during my years in Chicago. Shoot, the Sunday when Walter Payton broke Jimmy Brown's all-time rushing record—a decent October afternoon—there were seven thousand no-shows. Don't get me all wrong now. I run into hundreds and hundreds of people always saying, "You know, I've been a Bear season ticket holder for thirty years. . . ." I realize that a lot of fans in Chicago have endured a lot of bad teams in a lot of different sports, so maybe they're naturally a little skeptical by now. But, after the show we put on in 1985—not only going 18–1 but being entertaining, too—I think it's time for the people at least to give us the benefit of the doubt.

I'm not down on all fans any more than I'm down on all members of the press. I just feel there's a certain fair-weather attitude in both areas, and I have this sneaking suspicion that if we don't win every game or don't blow everybody out at the start of the 1986 regular season, they'll be down on us, particularly on the ever-popular quarterback, me.

I know that certain members of the media have been waiting for me to fail since I first showed my face in Chicago, and that's not going to change with a Super Bowl championship. They won't pick on Wally; he doesn't deserve to be picked on, anyway. They won't pick on anybody, but they'll fry me the first time I mess up. I know it, and I'm prepared for it. There will always be some degree of resentment for me, not only because I've won some ball games wherever I've played, but because of the way I act. That's a given. I'll be a fall guy until I start kissing some behinds. That means I'll always be a fall guy, because I'm never going to start kissing behinds. All of that will just make me play harder, of course.

I'm confident that feeling will be all around the locker room. I'm not the only player who noticed that the fans weren't behind us until the very end last year. I'm not the only player who felt that some writers and broadcasters were waiting for us to "choke." And from now on, I won't be the only player who will do his best to avoid having to hear about how we read all our press clippings, about how we got fat and sassy, about how we don't care anymore. First time we lose, we'll get it. Then again, what happens if we don't lose?

That's the sort of thing that makes every Sunday such a challenge. That's why I love a challenge. That's why I don't plan on letting any distractions get in our way. If the reflection from the huge, expensive diamond that Michael McCaskey gave us in our Super Bowl rings blinds us, we'll just have to put those suckers in the dresser drawers and get on with our priorities. They'll see how greedy we are, how self-satisfied we are, how content we are.

I know another thing. If Mike Ditka senses any bad vibes, he will go absolutely nuts. He will rant and rave like he's never ranted and raved. Please!! Anything but that. Let us be successful again.

If there's one change of pace that might be fun for this group of guys, besides winning a few more Super Bowls in a row, how about a game between the Bears' offense and the Bears' defense? Not a scrimmage like you see in training camp. I mean a real game. That would be wild. Our defense is great, but our offense knows where to attack it. There would be an awful lot of flags and fights, though. And they'd have to keep an ambulance close by. Come to think of it, that's not a great idea after all. They might never finish the game. Sorry I brought it up. Let's save our energy for Sundays.

As for myself off the field, I'll continue to fight for the Keith Van Hornes, the guys who slug it out and don't make nearly the money I've been lucky enough to make. I don't plan on doing a whole lot of work after I'm done with football. I might stay in the game as a scout or something. Never a coach. Point is, there are a lot of players, teammates I love and respect, who won't have that luxury. They'll have to rev it up and start work all over again, because their careers either weren't long enough or profitable enough for them to pick and choose. These things happen, though, when the NFL owners are going broke.

I'll butt heads with management, no doubt, even harder than I butt helmets with my teammates as a way to celebrate a touchdown. I suppose, as long as I'm around, management will be leery of me, not knowing what to expect. That's okay by me. Keep them guessing. I'll be there to play my damnedest on Sundays; none of the rest of this stuff really matters anyway, does it?

"What about movies?" I'm asked, when people probe into my future plans. Well, to tell you the truth, I haven't given much thought to what I'll be doing in twenty years. I'm not all that impressed by the celebrity scene, particularly if it means taking time away from things I'd rather do. I want to see my kids grow up healthy and aware. I don't want them to give anybody grief because their father happens to be a quarterback for the Bears. I don't want them to *take* any aggravation because of their father's occupation, either.

"You'll never want your kids saying some of the things

you say, will you?" Bears' general manager Jerry Vainisi asked me once.

"Damn right, I do," I said. "I want my kids to stick up for themselves, for what they think is right. I want to help them, but I want them to help themselves, too." How does that saying go? "If you give someone a fish, he'll eat for a day. If you teach him to fish, he'll eat for a lifetime."

I may be famous, but I'm a father and a husband first. Besides, I don't need to be a cover boy. I'd always wanted to be on the front of *Rolling Stone* magazine for some reason, and I made it right after the Super Bowl. But I wanted Van Horne and Kurt Becker on the front with me, and it didn't come out that way. The story was okay, but not the pictures. My friends are my friends, no matter what. We will always stick together.

I wouldn't mind meeting Jack Nicholson, though. I had a chance to when I was out in Los Angeles. He's a big Laker fan, and he was out at a basketball game when I told someone I'd like to shake his hand. Nicholson left word for me to come on out and drop by, but I didn't want to bother him. Someday, I will. *One Flew Over the Cuckoo's Nest* is my favorite film of all time. Nance finally bought it for me one Valentine's Day, so I could play it over and over again.

The first time I saw it was in 1976, I think. I was on my way to BYU, and the movie caught my attention. Nicholson played the part of Randle P. McMurphy, a patient in a mental institution. There was one catch. He was the sanest one of them all. He wasn't crazy. He wasn't going to give in to the little people, no matter what they thought of him, no matter how many times they told him he was wrong, no matter how many times they told him he was nuts. See what I'm getting at here?

Unfortunately, the story didn't end there. McMurphy finally had it up to here, so he went to strangle the zookeeper, a witch, Nurse Ratched. He almost got her . . . then they got him. They zapped him. They lobotomized him, took all the fight out of McMurphy, took all the McMurphy out of McMurphy. Chilling, but then, it was only a flick.

If they want to come after me like that, all these people who think I'm crazy, who think I'm a jerk, they'll know where to find me.

I'll be sitting in my recliner in my dream house. I'll have Ashley in one arm, Sean in another arm, I'll be hugging my wife, Nance, the greatest woman in the world . . . and I'll also be holding a beverage, probably a Moosehead.

I realize that's a lot of hands and arms, but like I was saying before, I'm not much for details. I'll work on that part of my game, though, and I'll get it down before we meet again, which we just might do.

To be continued. . . .

VITAL STATISTICS

JIM McMAHON

Ht: 6–1 Wt: 190 Born: 8/21/59 Jersey City, NJ

NCAA RECORDS

TOTAL OFFENSE (28)

1. Most yards gained (Half): 384 (vs. Texas-El Paso, Nov. 1)
2. Most yards gained (Season): 4,627
3. Most yards gained per game (Season): 385.6
4. Most yards gained (2 years): 8,085 (1980–1981)
5. Most yards gained in 2 Consecutive Games: 939 (423 vs. Wyoming, Oct. 11; 516 vs. Utah State, Oct. 18)
6. Most yards gained in 3 Consecutive Games: 1,365 (552 vs. Utah, Nov. 21; 274 vs. Hawaii, Nov. 14; 539 vs. Colorado State, Nov. 7)
7. Most yards gained in 4 Consecutive Games: 1,821 (516 vs. Utah State, Oct. 18; 392 vs. Hawaii, Oct. 25; 453 vs. Texas-El Paso, Nov. 1; 460 vs. North Texas State, Nov. 8)
8. Most Games gaining 300 yards or more (Season): 11
9. Most Consecutive Games gaining 300 yards or more (Season): 11
10. Most Consecutive Games gaining 300 yards or more (Career): 12
11. Most Games gaining 400 or more (Season): 6
12. Most Games gaining 400 or more (Career): 9
13. Most Consecutive Games gaining 400 yards or more (Season): 4
14. Most TDs Responsible for (Season): 53
15. Most Points Responsible for (Season): 322
16. Most Consecutive Games gaining 400 yards or more (Career): 4
17. Most TDs Responsible for (TDs scored and passed for) 3 years: 93
18. Most Points Responsible for (Points scored and passed for) 3 years: 562
19. Most Games gaining 300 yards or more (Career): 17
20. Most yards gained, three-year career: 9,640
21. Most yards gained against One Opponent (Career): 1,251 vs. Utah
22. Most yards gained, four-year career: 9,723
23. Most TDs Responsible for, 4 years: 94
24. Most Points Responsible for, 4 years: 568
25. Most TDs Responsible for, 2 years: 83
26. Most Points Responsible for, 2 years: 502
27. Most yards gained per game, two-year career: 367.5
28. Most plays, two-year career: 1,027

TOTAL OFFENSE RECORDS TIED (1)

1. Most Seasons gaining 2,500 yards or more: 2

PASSING (27)

1. Most yards gained (Half): 372 (vs. Texas-El Paso, Nov. 1)
2. Most yards gained (Season): 4,571
3. Most yards gained (2 Years): 8,125 (1980–1981)
4. Most yards gained per game (Season): 380.9
5. Most yards gained in 4 Consecutive Games: 1,789 (485 vs. Utah State, Oct. 18; 389 vs. Hawaii, Oct. 25; 451 vs. Texas-El Paso, Nov. 1; 464 vs. North Texas State, Nov. 8)
6. Most Games gaining 300 yards or more (Season): 11
7. Most Consecutive Games gaining 300 yards or more (Season): 11
8. Most Consecutive Games gaining 300 yards or more (Career): 12
9. Most Touchdown Passes (Season): 47
10. Most Touchdown Passes per game (Season): 3.92
11. Most Games gaining 200 yards or more (Season): 11
12. Most Consecutive Games gaining 200 yards or more (Season): 11
13. Highest passing efficiency rating points (Season): 176.9
14. Most Yards Per Pass Attempt (Season, Min. 200 atts.): 10.27 (445 for 4,571)
15. Most Yards Per Completion (Season, Min. 200 comps.): 16.10 (284 for 4,571)
16. Highest Percentage of Passes for Touchdowns (Season, Min. 300 atts.); 10.56 (47 on 445 atts.)
17. Most Consecutive Games gaining 200 yards or more (Career): 21
18. Most TD Passes (Career) 2 years: 77
19. Most Games gaining 300 yards or more (Career): 17
20. Most yards gained, Three-year Career: 9,443
21. Most Touchdown Passes, Three-year Career: 83
22. Most passes completed, one game: 44
23. Highest passing efficiency, Career: 156.9
24. Most yards gained passing, Four-years (Career): 9,536
25. Most Touchdown Passes, Four-years (Career): 84
26. Most passes completed, Three-years (Career): 643
27. Most yards gained passing, 3 Consecutive Games: 1,372 (565 vs. Utah, 269 vs. Hawaii, 538 vs. Colorado State)

McMAHON COLLEGE RECORD GAME-BY-GAME

		RUSHING					PASSING					
DATE	OPPONENT	CARRIES	GAIN	LOSS	NET	TD	ATT.	COMP.	INT.	YARDS	TD	PCT.
9/10/77	Kansas State	(Punted Only)										
9/24	Utah State	1	0	0	0	0	1	1	0	6	0	1000
9/30	New Mexico	(Punted Only)										
10/8	Oregon State	(Punted Only)										
10/15	Colorado St	3	3	23	−20	0	3	2	1	14	0	.667
10/22	Wyoming	(Punted Only)										
10/29	Arizona	0	0	0	0	0	3	1	0	6	0	.333
11/5	Utah	0	0	0	0	0	2	2	0	12	0	1000
11/12	Arizona St	(Punted Only)										
11/19	Long Beach	2	0	15	−15	0	0	0	0	0	0	—
11/26	Tex-El Paso	1	15	0	15	0	7	4	0	65	1	.571
TOTALS:		**7**	**18**	**38**	**−20**	**0**	**16**	**10**	**1**	**103**	**1**	**.625**
9/9/78	Oregon St	(Punted Only)										
9/16	Arizona St	(Punted Only)										
9/23	Colorado St	12	90	10	80	1	9	7	1	112	1	.778
9/30	New Mexico	(Punted Only)										
10/7	Utah State	13	83	12	71	0	11	5	1	62	0	.454
10/14	Oregon	6	18	8	10	0	19	10	0	204	1	.526
10/21	Tex-El Paso	20	85	23	62	0	19	10	1	143	1	.526
11/4	Wyoming	13	54	5	49	2	36	24	1	317	1	.667
11/11	San Diego St	17	31	54	−23	1	29	11	3	174	1	.379
11/18	Utah	12	76	64	12	0	38	15	0	249	1	.395
11/25	Hawaii	(Did not play—injured)										
12/2	Nev-Las Vegas	6	7	20	−13	0	15	5	1	46	0	.333
TOTALS:		**99**	**444**	**196**	**248**	**4**	**176**	**87**	**8**	**1,307**	**6**	**.494**
	McMahon Red-Shirted the 1979 Season											
9/6/80	New Mexico	11	11	55	−44	0	25	11	1	147	2	.440
9/13	San Diego	4	2	9	−7	0	30	19	1	373	4	.663
9/20	Wisconsin	5	12	9	3	1	34	22	0	337	3	.647
9/27	Long Beach	13	32	46	−14	0	42	25	1	339	4	.595
10/11	Wyoming	4	15	0	15	0	31	22	2	408	4	.710
10/18	Utah State	10	40	9	31	2	33	21	3	485	6	.636
10/25	Hawaii	8	23	20	3	0	60	31	3	389	2	.517
11/1	Tex-El Paso	2	12	10	2	0	36	28	1	451	6	.778
11/8	No. Texas St	8	24	28	−4	0	50	40	3	464	3	.800
11/15	Colorado St	10	35	34	1	0	33	23	1	441	5	.697

Vital Statistics

		RUSHING					PASSING					
DATE	OPPONENT	CARRIES	GAIN	LOSS	NET	TD	ATT.	COMP.	INT.	YARDS	TD	PCT.
11/22	Utah	8	53	26	27	1	34	21	1	399	3	.618
11/29	Nev-Las Vegas	12	84	41	43	2	37	21	1	338	5	.568
TOTALS:		**95**	**343**	**287**	**56**	**6**	**445**	**284**	**18**	**4,571**	**47**	**.638**
9/5/81	Long Beach	8	17	17	0	0	45	28	2	403	0	.622
9/12	Air Force	8	20	15	5	0	39	28	0	226	4	.718
9/19	Tex-El Paso	5	12	16	−4	0	31	21	0	267	4	.656
9/26	Colorado	4	21	3	18	0	30	15	0	263	3	.500
10/2	Utah State	(Did not play—injured)										
10/10	Nev-Las Vegas	(Did not play—injured)										
10/17	San Diego St	7	1	41	−40	0	42	27	2	349	3	.643
10/24	Wyoming	8	13	48	−35	0	47	29	1	393	2	.617
10/31	New Mexico	7	6	40	−34	0	37	23	0	282	3	.622
11/7	Colorado State	3	9	8	1	0	65	44	1	538	7	.677
11/14	Hawaii	9	22	17	5	0	33	22	1	269	0	.677
11/21	Utah	5	9	22	−13	0	54	35	0	565	4	.648
TOTALS:		**64**	**130**	**227**	**−97**	**0**	**423**	**272**	**7**	**3,555**	**30**	**.643**
CAREER TOTALS:		**265**	**935**	**748**	**187**	**10**	**1060**	**653**	**34**	**9,536**	**84**	**.616**

Longest Scoring Pass	80 vs.	SDSU (1980)
Longest Non-Scoring Pass	71 vs.	Wyoming (1978)
Most Passes Attempted	65 vs.	Colorado St. (1981)
Most Pass Completions	44 vs.	Colorado St. (1981)
Most Pass Interceptions	3 vs.	Three teams
Most Yards Passing	565 vs.	Utah (1981)
Most Touchdown Passes	7 vs.	Colorado St. (1981)
Most Net Yards Rushing	80 vs.	Colorado St. (1978)
Most Yards Total Offense	552 vs.	Utah (1981)
Most Punts in one game	12 vs.	Oregon St. (1978)
Longest Punt	58 vs.	Colorado St. (1978)
Best One-Game Punting Ave.	46.3 vs.	Colorado St. (1978)
Best Completion Percentage	80%	(40 of 50) vs. NTS (1980)

Total Number of Games Played—44
Number of Games Missed—3 (Hawaii, 1978—back injury; USU, UNLV, 1981—knee injury)
Number of Games Punted—8 (five in 1977, three in 1978)

1981 AP 1st Team All-America
UPI 1st Team All-America
Football Coaches 1st Team All-America
Football Writers 1st Team All-America
Football News 1st Team All-America
Mizlou/Hartford Insurance 1st Team All-America
NEA 2nd Team All-America
College and Pro Football Newsweekly 2nd Team All-America
Sporting News Honorable Mention All-America
1st Team All-Western Athletic Conference (WAC)
WAC Offensive Player-of-the-Year
Washington Pigskin Club Offensive Player-of-the-Year
ABC-TV/Chevrolet Player-of-the-Game vs. San Diego State
Sports Illustrated Player-of-the-Week vs. Colorado State
Playboy Preseason All-America
Street and Smith Honorable Mention Preseason All-America
Street and Smith All-Rookie Preseason Team
'82 Hula Bowl
'82 Senior Bowl
'82 Olympia Gold Bowl

1980 Football Coaches 1st Team All-America
College and Pro Football Newsweekly 1st Team All-America
AP 2nd Team All-America
UPI 2nd Team All-America
Football News 2nd Team All-America
Sporting News Honorable Mention All-America
1st Team All-WAC
WAC Player-of-the-Year
Utah Sportsman-of-the-Year
Deseret News Athlete-of-the-Year
Holiday Bowl Co-Offensive MVP
ABC-TV/Chevrolet Player-of-the-Game vs. San Diego State, Utah State
Sports Illustrated Player-of-the-Week vs. Utah State
WAC Player-of-the-Week vs. San Diego, Wyoming, Utah State

1978 AP Honorable Mention All-America
1st Team All-WAC
ABC-TV/Chevrolet Player-of-the-Game vs. Colorado State
WAC Player-of-the-Week vs. Colorado State, Wyoming

Statistics courtesy of Brigham Young University

McMAHON PRO STATS

YEAR/ CLUB	GMS/STS	PASSING ATT	COM	PCT	YDS	INT	TDS	RATING	RUSHING ATT	YDS	AVG	TD
1985 Bears	13/11	313	178	56.9	2,392	11	15	82.8	47	252	5.4	3
1984 Bears	9/9	143	85	59.4	1,146	2	8	97.8	39	276	7.1	2
1983 Bears	14/13	295	175	59.3	2,184	13	12	77.7	55	307	5.6	2
1982 Bears	8/7	210	120	57.1	1,501	7	9	80.1	25	105	4.4	1
CAREER	**44/40**	**961**	**558**	**58.1**	**7,223**	**33**	**44**	**83.0**	**166**	**940**	**5.7**	**8**

McMAHON PRO RECORD GAME-BY-GAME

DATE	OPPONENT	ATT	COMP	INT	YDS	TD	PCT	SACKED/ YDS LST	LONG GAIN
9/12/82	@DETROIT	. . . . DNP							
9/19	NEW ORLEANS	22	12	1	131	0	54.5	4/33	24
	7-GAME STRIKE								
11/21	DETROIT	27	16	3	233	2	59.3	3/12	44
11/28	@MINNESOTA	20	12	1	139	1	60.0	7/56	50
12/5	NEW ENGLAND	21	15	1	192	2	71.4	3/16	40
12/12	@SEATTLE	29	19	1	199	0	65.5	2/25	29
12/19	ST. LOUIS	33	16	0	160	1	48.5	1/5	45
12/26	@L.A. RAMS	28	18	0	280	2	64.3	2/17	40
1/2/83	@TAMPA BAY	30	12	0	167	1	40.0	4/32	31
9/4/83	ATLANTA	29	20	1	254	1	69.0	4/22	34
9/11	TAMPA BAY	24	16	2	286	1	66.7	4/23	73
9/18	@NEW ORLEANS	17	11	1	172	1	64.7	5/41	60
9/25	@BALTIMORE	20	8	0	89	0	40.0	3/15	26
10/2	DENVER	23	15	3	174	1	65.2	0/0	52
10/9	MINNESOTA	11	4	2	35	0	36.4	2/13	12
10/16	@DETROIT	. . . . DNP							
10/23	@PHILADELPHIA	. . . . DNP							
10/30	DETROIT	16	11	0	126	1	68.8	0/0	21
11/6	@L.A. RAMS	29	19	1	178	0	65.5	4/26	28
11/13	PHILADELPHIA	16	10	0	140	2	62.5	4/28	43
11/20	@TAMPA BAY	12	8	0	79	0	66.7	1/6	22
11/27	SAN FRANCISCO	19	11	0	159	1	57.9	4/26	49
1/24	GREEN BAY	38	20	1	298	1	52.6	4/24	87
12/11	@MINNESOTA	16	8	0	32	1	50.0	2/13	8
12/18	GREEN BAY	25	14	2	162	2	56.0	5/29	35

DATE	OPPONENT	ATT	COMP	INT	YDS	TD	PCT	SACKED/ YDS LST	LONG GAIN
9/2/84	TAMPA BAY	22	16	1	138	1	72.7	1/3	21
9/9	DENVER	8	5	0	93	1	62.5	0/0	61
9/16	@GREEN BAY	7	4	0	39	0	57.1	0/0	20
9/23	@SEATTLE	. . .	. . .	. . .	. . .	DNP	. . .	. . .	. . .
9/30	DALLAS	14	6	0	79	0	42.9	2/5	22
10/7	NEW ORLEANS	14	10	0	128	1	71.4	4/31	23
10/14	@ST. LOUIS	23	13	0	202	1	56.5	1/4	36
10/21	@TAMPA BAY	18	12	0	219	3	66.7	1/3	49
10/28	MINNESOTA	26	16	0	180	1	61.5	1/2	40
11/4	L.A. RAIDERS	11	3	1	68	0	27.3	0/0	50
	INJURED RESERVE REMAINDER OF SEASON (1984)								
9/8/85	TAMPA BAY	34	23	1	274	2	67.6	3/23	27
9/15	NEW ENGLAND	21	13	1	232	1	61.9	1/6	49
9/19	@MINNESOTA	15	8	0	236	3	53.3	0/0	70
9/29	WASHINGTON	19	13	1	160	3	68.4	2/6	33
10/6	@TAMPA BAY	34	22	2	292	1	64.7	1/6	48
10/13	@SAN FRANCISCO	31	18	1	186	0	58.1	1/3	34
10/21	GREEN BAY	26	12	0	144	0	46.2	2/3	23
10/27	MINNESOTA	31	18	1	181	2	58.1	0/0	33
11/3	@GREEN BAY	20	9	0	91	1	45.0	4/33	21
11/10	DETROIT	. . .	. . .	. . .	. . .	DNP	. . .	. . .	. . .
11/17	@DALLAS	. . .	. . .	. . .	. . .	DNP	. . .	. . .	. . .
11/24	ATLANTA	. . .	. . .	. . .	. . .	DNP	. . .	. . .	. . .
12/2	@MIAMI	6	3	1	42	0	50.0	2/14	20
12/8	INDIANAPOLIS	23	11	0	145	0	47.8	3/8	30
12/14	@N.Y. JETS	31	15	1	215	1	48.4	5/12	65
12/22	@DETROIT	22	13	2	194	1	59.1	3/18	37
	PLAYOFFS	**ATT**	**COMP**	**INT**	**TDS**	**TD**	**PCT**	**TKLD/ LST**	**LONG GAIN**
1/5/86	N.Y. GIANTS	21	11	0	216	2	52.4	0/0	46
1/12	L.A. RAMS	25	16	0	164	1	64.0	3/23	22
1/26	NEW ENGLAND	20	12	0	256	0	60.0	1/3	60
	@NEW ORLEANS								

McMAHON vs. NFL REGULAR SEASON (PASSING)

OPPONENT	GMS	ATT	COMP	YDS	TD	INT	PCT
ATLANTA	1	29	20	254	1	1	69.0
DALLAS	1	14	6	79	0	0	42.9
DENVER	2	31	20	267	2	3	64.5
DETROIT	3	65	40	553	4	5	61.5
GREEN BAY	5	116	59	734	4	3	50.9
INDIANAPOLIS	2	43	19	234	0	0	44.2
L.A. RAMS	2	57	37	458	2	1	64.9
L.A. RAIDERS	1	11	3	68	0	1	27.3
MIAMI	1	6	3	42	0	1	50.0
MINNESOTA	6	119	66	803	8	4	55.5
NEW ENGLAND	2	42	28	424	3	2	66.7
NEW ORLEANS	3	53	33	431	2	2	62.3
N.Y. JETS	1	31	15	215	1	1	48.4
PHILADELPHIA	1	16	10	140	2	0	62.5
ST. LOUIS	2	56	29	362	2	0	51.8
SAN FRANCISCO	2	50	29	345	1	1	58.0
SEATTLE	1	29	19	199	0	1	65.5
TAMPA BAY	7	174	109	1,455	9	6	62.6
WASHINGTON	1	19	13	160	3	1	68.4

1985 SEASON: Emerged as one of NFL's top quarterbacks while earning first Pro Bowl appearance . . . Started 11 regular season games and all three post-season contests . . . Averaged 64% completion first 5 weeks before injury woes began at S.F. (10/17) . . . Threw career high 15 TD passes . . . Threw 9 TD passes in first 4 games . . . Led team with 5.4 yard rushing average . . . Missed three games (11/10–11/24) with shoulder tendonitis and did not start vs. Vikes (9/19) due to stiff neck . . . Entered Vikes game in 3rd quarter and put on one of best shows of NFL '85 season throwing TD passes on first two plays and three in just 1½ quarters to turn 17-9 deficit into 33-24 win (8-15-236) . . . Named NFC offensive player-of-the-week in season opener after 23 of 34 for 274-yard, 2 TD effort in 38-28 win over Bucs . . . Passed for season-high 292 yards at Tampa (10/6) on 22 of 34 performance . . . Completed 13 of 19 passes for 160 yards and 3 TD's; caught TD pass from Payton and rushed for 36 yards vs. Redskins (9/29) . . . Threw 3 TD passes in playoffs and scored first TD vs. Rams on 16-yard run . . . Did not throw interception in 3 post-season games in 66 attempts . . . Super Bowl performance included 12 of 20 for 256 yards.
GAMES PLAYED: 13. **GAMES STARTED:** 11.

PRO CAREER: Has led Bears to victory in 26 of his last 30 starts . . . Game ball performance at Tampa (10/21/84) after throwing 3 TD's and completing 12 of 18 for 219 yards . . . Set Bears record in '83 for completion percentage (58.4) . . . Passed for career-high 298 yards at Green Bay (12/4/83) . . . Had 3,200+ yard passing games in '83 and threw longest pass in NFC that year with 87-yard TD strike to Gault at Green Bay (12/4/83) . . . Voted UPI NFC "Rookie of the Year" in '82 . . . Professional Football Writers' Association, Pro Football Weekly, and Football Digest all-rookie selection . . . 80.1 passing rating in '82 was 4th in NFC, 9th in NFL, 8th best in Bear history, best in NFL for a rookie . . . Earned game ball as rookie vs. Lions (12/21/82) after completing 16 of 27 for 233 yards, 2 TD . . . Earned Brian Piccolo Award in '82 after starting 7 games.

Statistics courtesy of the Chicago Bears

McMAHON CHARITIES

Juvenile Diabetes Foundation

Hands Across America

Special Olympics
(honorary coach)

Cancer Treatment Center

American Kidney Foundation

Sunshine Foundation
(terminal children)

National Sports Chairman of
Children's Miracle Network

Sports Aide

POW—MIA

Children's Hospital

National Football League
Pro Quarterback of the Year
of the Washington Quarterback Club,
benefiting Cystic Fibrosis

National Multiple Sclerosis
Honorary Chairman, M-S Read-a-thon

Society to Prevent Blindness

National Handicap Sports Association